AMERICAN HORTICULTURAL SOCIETY
PRACTICAL GUIDES

WATER-WISE
GARDENING

AMERICAN HORTICULTURAL SOCIETY
PRACTICAL GUIDES

WATER-WISE
GARDENING

Peter Robinson

www.dk.com.

A DK PUBLISHING BOOK
www.dk.com

SERIES EDITOR Pamela Brown
SERIES ART EDITOR Stephen Josland
ART EDITOR Rachael Parfitt
US EDITOR Ray Rogers

MANAGING EDITOR Louise Abbott
MANAGING ART EDITOR Lee Griffiths

DTP DESIGNER Matthew Greenfield

PRODUCTION Ruth Charlton, Mandy Inness

First American Edition, 1999
2 4 6 8 10 9 7 5 3 1

Published in the United States by
DK Publishing, Inc., 95 Madison Avenue, New York, New York 10016

Library of Congress Cataloging-in-Publication data

Water-wise gardening. -- 1st American ed.
    p.   cm.   --   (AHS practical guides)
Includes index.
ISBN 0-7894-4161-6 (alk. paper)
1. Landscape gardening--Water conservation
I. DK Publishing, Inc.   II. Series.
SB475.83.W38 1999
635.9'5--dc21   98-48211
                                                                  CIP

Reproduced by Colourscan, Singapore
Printed and bound by Star Standard Industries, Singapore

CONTENTS

SAVING WATER IN THE GARDEN

LOOKING TO THE FUTURE

EACH YEAR, RAINFALL RECORDS around the world emphasize just how unpredictable weather can be. What is certain, though, is that the daily, ever-rising demand for water means that gardeners everywhere need to think carefully about how they use – and sometimes waste – this precious and limited resource and how, with a little imagination, they can easily help conserve it.

A CHANGE OF DIRECTION

Drought is relative – meaning different things in different parts of the world. But almost everywhere, water now has its price, both economically and, more importantly, in terms of the environment. Even in temperate regions, gardeners are facing prolonged shortages and can no longer simply turn on the hose. For some, saving water may only involve introducing ways of storing rainwater and improving moisture conservation in the soil. For others, it is providing the impetus for change to a more inventive approach, planting only drought-tolerant plants or even looking for inspiration to the dry areas of the globe where ornament and structure play a key role. All these ideas are helping pave the way for more ecologically conscious gardens in the 21st century.

BLUE AND GREEN
A mosaic pool and brightly painted walls are the dominant features in this tiny courtyard garden. A cleverly placed mirror makes the garden appear larger than it really is, as well as making the planting look more luxuriant.

◄WHERE THE WIND BLOWS *Grasses, broom, and* Anthemis *stand up to wind and scarcity of water.*

OLD STYLE, NEW METHODS

Even in the most conventional garden, simple changes in cultivation techniques and planting ideas can be extremely effective without drastically affecting style. Mulches (*see p.22*) help limit evaporation from the soil, water barrels or tanks (*see p.45*) can be used to store rainwater during times of plenty, and, if need be, household waste water can be recycled. Small shade trees help provide cooler pockets of air, and windbreaks (*see p.15*) greatly reduce the drying effect of wind. When combined with suitable plants (*see pp.29–37*), using only a few of these methods will cut down on the need for supplementary watering. On the other hand, this may be the time to take a more fundamental look at your garden design.

MEDITERRANEAN EFFECT

In Mediterranean countries, it was realized long ago that even in a hot, dry climate, gardens could offer shade and refreshment yet use a minimum of water. These small walled gardens and courtyards, often of Moorish influence, have had an enormous impact on garden design, particularly in countries sharing a similar climate. The emphasis is on minimal planting, usually in conjunction with a water feature such as a fountain or canal, with great importance placed on the mix of colors and textures of

---

For a superb design source, look at what works in the wild

---

nonplant materials. This is a style that has become popular in colder climates, too, especially in small city gardens, where it is possible to recreate an enclosed atmosphere. Wall fountains, raised pools, and small canals that rely on small submersible pumps for recirculation use very little water.

SWATHS OF COLOR
Yellow yarrow, red Lychnis, *and red-hot pokers* (Kniphofia) *combine in a planting that, once established, needs little additional watering.*

◀ BARE MINIMUM
In this Australian garden, the minimalist approach has been taken to the extreme, with cacti alone forming the planting. It would be easy to introduce a water feature and shading for the seating.

▼ ON THE BEACH
In his inimitable garden in the gravel of the Kent coast, artist Derek Jarman mixed seashore flotsam with native British species and California poppies (Eschscholzia).

PRAIRIE THEME

In complete contrast to the courtyards of the Mediterranean are the informal "naturalistic" gardens inspired by the dry expanses and prairies of most continents. This type of landscape is often dominated by wild grasses and scrub, punctuated by scatterings of wildflowers. When copied in gardens, the effect can be extremely successful. Plants will need watering until they are settled in, but thereafter this type of planting places little dependence on extra water. Under a less brilliant sun, the colors have a pleasing harmony in both winter and summer and, in wind, the light, often feathery flowers have a soothing quality. With this kind of style, it is not essential to look too far from home for planting ideas. You can use drought-tolerant native species in a design that blends with local landscapes, or you may have the best of both worlds, creating just this type of effect (*see pp.18 and 30*) but including plants that have been bred for improved flower, color, length of season, or sometimes resistance to disease.

ASSESSING THE PROBLEMS

WHEN STARTING A NEW GARDEN, or redesigning or deciding the best way to reduce water consumption in an existing garden, it is important to assess just how much of a problem you face. Many factors affect the rate at which a garden may lose or use water, and that in turn may vary in different parts of the same site. Soil type, wind, sun, and shade all play their part, as well as the frequency with which the rain clouds gather.

THE RAIN FACTOR

The amount of rain a garden receives is inevitably the major factor influencing the need to conserve water and your choice of design and plants. Different regions receiving the same total annual rainfall may face very different problems. The effect of small regular amounts will not be the same as that of infrequent but heavy storms or the majority of the rain falling in one season, and plants have developed a wide variety of adaptations to suit conditions. Where annual rainfall is generally below 18in (45cm), lawns will wither without irrigation, and plants should be limited to those that can resist drought (*see pp.32–35*). An inexpensive gauge will record just how much rain any garden receives (and also if the amount varies within the same garden, due to tree cover or rainshadow).

LUXURY LAWNS
A garden that relies for effect on immaculately mown grass and a profusion of leafy, well-nourished plants is bound to be one of the first to suffer in prolonged periods of drought unless it can be given a supplementary supply of water. In areas where water is limited, a verdant lawn may need to be regarded as dispensable and replaced by gravel or other hard landscaping (see p.24).

OTHER ELEMENTAL EFFECTS

Next to rainfall, soil type has the greatest impact on the amount of water available to plants (*see p.20*). In areas of low rainfall, a garden with clay soil will usually support a different and much wider range of plants than a fast-draining sandy or gravelly soil. Soil depth also affects moisture retention; in regions with alkaline soil, there is often only a thin layer of soil over an underlying rocky layer, severely limiting the amount of water that can be retained. Soils with a naturally high organic content, such as peaty soils, are less likely to be a problem, since peat retains water.

Although in many temperate regions wind is often associated with driving rain, its general effect is to desiccate foliage, especially if it is persistent. Not only does wind increase evaporation from the soil surface, it also dramatically increases the rate of transpiration, and this loss of water from leaves in turn places a greater demand for water on plant roots. Erecting windbreaks to counter prevailing winds or temporarily screening vulnerable new plantings will help (*see p.15*).

Sunshine and shade can both add their own problems. In bright sunlight, even when temperatures are on the cool side, the rate of photosynthesis (the process by which plants manufacture the substances that they need for growth) rises, and more moisture is lost in the process. Glare caused by extensive paved areas and reflective, light-colored walls exaggerates the effect of the sun. Trees help create cool shade, but the soil underneath is likely to be dry because of the umbrella effect of their canopies and their thirsty, extensive root systems.

PAVING THE WAY
A strong design that depends on attractive structural features will demand far less water than one centered around thirsty grass and lush borders. Here, vertical screens and pergolas help reduce the drying effects of wind; decking and gravel reduce evaporation from the ground; and drought-resistant plants are used to good effect in raised beds and wooden planters.

TYPICAL TROUBLESPOTS

A BIRD'S-EYE VIEW OF THE AVERAGE BACKYARD quickly reveals not only those features that demand, or waste, the most water but also how opportunities for saving it can easily be missed. In this yard, large amounts of rainwater could be collected from the roofs of both house and shed and stored in a barrel (*see p.45*). This, in turn, could be used to water containers, especially hanging baskets, and the vegetable patch, and to fill up a pond if necessary.

WHERE THE WATER DISAPPEARS

A large percentage of water, of course, simply disappears into thin air – lost through evaporation. Surfaces, therefore, are one of the first areas to look at for ways of saving moisture. A good thick mulch (*see p.22*) laid between flowers, shrubs, and vegetables while the soil is damp is invaluable in helping to conserve moisture in beds and borders. Mulches are just as useful, too, in containers where they can add to the decorative effect (*see p.39*).

Lawns are the thirstiest surfaces of all. Water is lost through transpiration from each and every blade of grass. Choose appropriate grasses (*see p.27*) and mow less frequently. Under trees it is often best to concede the battle and use drought-tolerant groundcover plants (*see p.34*).

To prevent rainwater from disappearing from patios straight into the soil, give paved areas a gentle slope toward the lawn and, if appropriate, the pond. Permeable areas between slabs or bricks allow water to seep through and reach the roots of plants that extend beneath. Wooden decking offers the same advantage (*see p.25*).

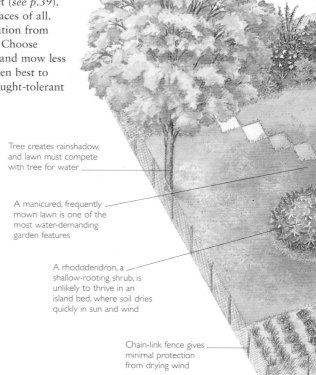

POTENTIAL PROBLEMS

• Wire fencing on boundary offers little protection from drying wind.
• Bare soil will lose moisture in sparsely planted beds.
• The lawn will be an early victim of drought and soon turn brown without supplementary watering.
• Hanging baskets and widely spaced containers need frequent watering.
• Fountain and pond will lose water, especially through evaporation.

Tree creates rainshadow, and lawn must compete with tree for water

A manicured, frequently mown lawn is one of the most water-demanding garden features

A rhododendron, a shallow-rooting shrub, is unlikely to thrive in an island bed, where soil dries quickly in sun and wind

Chain-link fence gives minimal protection from drying wind

APPROPRIATE PLANTING

Modifying the choice of plants helps save water. Avoid notoriously thirsty trees such as willow and poplar. Similarly, exchange pole beans for less water-demanding root vegetables and onions, and forego delphiniums in favor of drought-resistant flowers such as hollyhocks. Specimen plants in the center of a lawn or in single containers on a patio lose more moisture than if they are part of a group planting. All plants will benefit from some form of screen that reduces wind (*see p.15*).

SIMPLE REMEDIES

• Erect a type of fencing that will act as a windbreak, and install water barrels.
• Mulch bare soil and start a compost pile. Use compost to improve soil's water retention.
• Do not cut grass too closely, and/or reduce lawn size or replace with a different surface.
• Incorporate water-retaining granules into the soil mix in pots and hanging baskets.
• Use a heavier, single-spout fountain, or dispense with it and plant waterlilies to cover pool surface and reduce evaporation.

Bed contains plants such as delphiniums and *Ligularia* with large, soft leaves that soon wilt in dry spells. Bare soil, created by sparse planting, loses moisture through evaporation

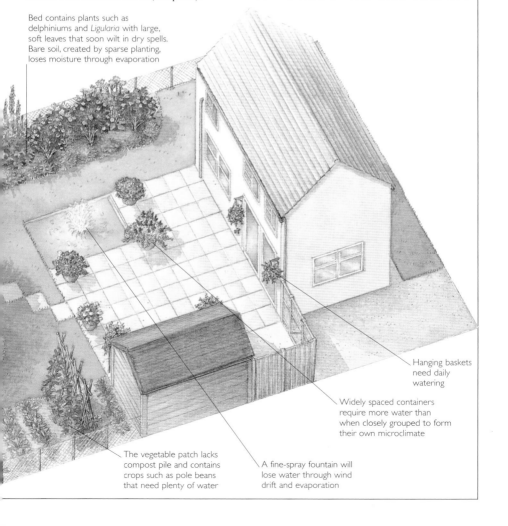

Hanging baskets need daily watering

Widely spaced containers require more water than when closely grouped to form their own microclimate

The vegetable patch lacks compost pile and contains crops such as pole beans that need plenty of water

A fine-spray fountain will lose water through wind drift and evaporation

SOME BASIC SOLUTIONS

A GARDEN'S POTENTIAL FOR SAVING WATER can often be improved gradually, but some fundamental decisions may be required at the outset. Very windy sites, especially near the coast, are likely to need a shelterbelt of trees and shrubs, which takes time to establish (*see p.34*), although an easily erected artificial windbreak solves the problem in many gardens. A slope is often a more difficult problem; on steep sites, terracing is the only answer.

COPING WITH SLOPES

On slopes, water runs off quickly and has much less opportunity to be absorbed by the soil. Where plants are not being planted in great number or in rows, form a shallow depression in the soil around each plant that can act like an individual reservoir (*see p.44*). This is particularly beneficial for shrubs and trees. On a steep slope, however, in order to create reasonably level planting areas, terracing may need to be carried out and, if necessary, retaining walls built. Where there is hardly any topsoil and the bedrock is exposed, planting will need to be limited to rock plants, which are superbly adapted to grow in this

> ## Terracing gives the soil a chance to absorb as much rain as possible

type of terrain. Sometimes there is so little soil for the plants to gain a foothold that the only solution is to sow seed *in situ*, enabling the developing plant to squeeze its roots into any available fissures in the rock.

AT THE ROCK FACE
Sempervivum, *adept at finding moisture in tiny cracks, are the perfect plant for clothing a rocky slope. After planting, some temporary netting will help hold the plants in place.*

WILLOW AND WOOD
Woven willow (left) *makes a good short-term windbreak, ideal for sheltering shrubs as they grow to form their own barrier. Spaced wooden laths* (below) *are effective and create dramatic shadows in winter.*

FILTERING THE WIND

Windbreaks of various forms should be considered carefully, particularly in temperate climates where drying wind is a factor all year. Even if windbreaks such as ranch-style fencing (*see below right*) are obtrusive at first, when used to support plants they add a new dimension to the garden planting.

Windbreaks are more effective when they filter wind rather than block it. A solid windbreak, such as a close-boarded fence, creates turbulence and eddying on the leeward side, which can cause a surprising amount of damage. Semipermeable artificial windbreaks, however, can be decorative in their own right. A trellis painted in a compatible color makes a good garden feature at the same time as reducing wind. Any wood should be pressure-treated and supported by strong pressure-treated posts. These could be made of concrete in extremely exposed positions.

The ideal permeability of a windbreak needs to be about 50 percent. This can be achieved by making panels of vertical wooden laths, approximately 1in (2.5cm) wide, with gaps in between of the same width. A windbreak's height is generally determined by the other features in a garden, but even a low trellis fence will reduce wind at ground level by some 7–10 times its own height. Added to this is the bonus that the windbreak can help reduce the sun's glare, particularly if some small ornamental trees are planted alongside.

GOOD WINDBREAKS

- Panels made of vertical 1in (2.5cm) wooden laths with small gaps in between.
- Horizontal ranch-style (baffle) fencing, using lumber 6in (15cm) wide with 6in (15cm) gaps.
- A trellis with a 6in (15cm) grid.
- Woven twig hurdles.
- Plastic windbreak netting (available in various colors and thicknesses).
- Rolls of split bamboo attached to upright frames.
- Evergreen hedges such as holly (*Ilex*).
- Deciduous hedges such as hawthorn (*Crataegus*) or sea buckthorn (*Hippophae*).

IMPROVING SOIL AND SURFACES

CONSERVING EVERY BIT OF WATER in the soil must be one of the main aims of the water-conscious gardener. This is best achieved by improving the soil's structure and covering its surface. Mulches may be restricted to beds and borders, but if you use a material such as gravel, which is decorative and easy to maintain, it can introduce a style to the garden that is so successful it does away entirely with the moisture-demanding, time-consuming lawn.

MAKING A GRAVEL GARDEN

Gravel blends beautifully with many drought-resistant plants and encourages a freer and more ecologically sensible gardening style. For maximum water conservation, lay the gravel over a sheet mulch (*see p.23*). But one of the charms of gravel is the way it allows plants to self-seed. For this to happen, lay it over lightly firmed soil, before or after planting. The plan on the next page uses plants that thrive in the conditions that gravel creates. The gravel soon becomes less noticeable as the plants develop, their growth speeded by being given a cool root run. In winter, it will also protect the lower leaves of gray-foliaged plants from excess winter moisture.

1 **Scoop the gravel** from the planting area, if planting after the gravel is laid, and put to one side so that it does not fall into the planting hole.

2 **Having made** a good-sized planting hole, add some compost and lightly tease out the plant's roots. Plant it level with the surrounding gravel.

3 **Fill the hole** with soil, as necessary, and firm the plant in. Water it well. Brush the gravel back under the leaves and around the stem.

◄TEXTURAL COMBINATION *Giant* Crambe *leaves contrast with the button flowers of* Santolina.

PLAN FOR A GRAVEL GARDEN

Light-reflecting gravel sets off silvery plants to perfection. In this plan (shown in late summer), aromatic lavender and *Santolina* will scent the air for months, while the *Euphorbia* sprawls languidly near their feet.

Little bluestem grass adds texture and sound when it rustles in the breeze. Although you will want some plants to self-seed, especially verbena, pull up unwanted taprooted *Eryngium* while small to avoid disturbing the gravel.

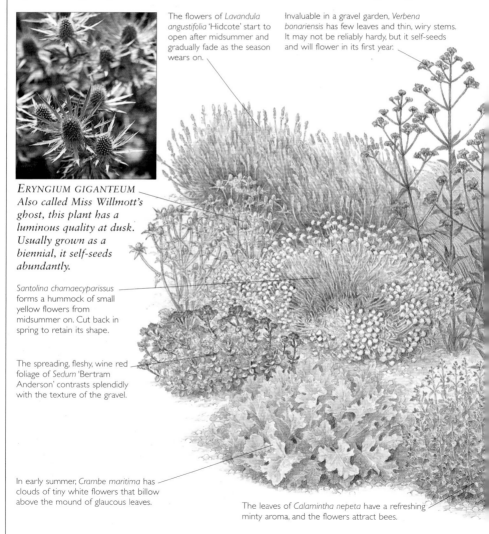

The flowers of *Lavandula angustifolia* 'Hidcote' start to open after midsummer and gradually fade as the season wears on.

Invaluable in a gravel garden, *Verbena bonariensis* has few leaves and thin, wiry stems. It may not be reliably hardy, but it self-seeds and will flower in its first year.

ERYNGIUM GIGANTEUM
Also called Miss Willmott's ghost, this plant has a luminous quality at dusk. Usually grown as a biennial, it self-seeds abundantly.

Santolina chamaecyparissus forms a hummock of small yellow flowers from midsummer on. Cut back in spring to retain its shape.

The spreading, fleshy, wine red foliage of *Sedum* 'Bertram Anderson' contrasts splendidly with the texture of the gravel.

In early summer, *Crambe maritima* has clouds of tiny white flowers that billow above the mound of glaucous leaves.

The leaves of *Calamintha nepeta* have a refreshing minty aroma, and the flowers attract bees.

PLANTING PLAN

1 2 *Lavandula angustifolia* 'Hidcote', 24 in (60cm) apart
2 3 *Eryngium giganteum*, informally arranged
3 1 *Santolina chamaecyparissus*
4 1 *Sedum* 'Bertram Anderson'
5 1 *Crambe maritima*
6 1 *Calamintha nepeta*
7 3 *Verbena bonariensis*, 30in (75cm) apart
8 3 *Schizachyrium scoparium*, 18in (45cm) apart
9 3 *Perovskia* 'Hybrida', 24in (60cm) apart
10 1 *Helianthemum apenninum*
11 1 *Euphorbia myrsinites*

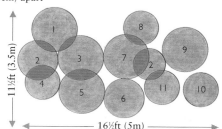

11½ft (3.5m)

16½ft (5m)

Schizachyrium scoparium is a highly drought-resistant grass, native to North American prairies.

Perovskia 'Hybrida' has aromatic foliage. The blue flowers appear in late summer.

MORE CHOICES

Artemisia 'Powis Castle'
Ballota pseudodictamnus
Erysimum 'Bowles' Mauve'
Eschscholzia californica
Festuca glauca
Gaura lindheimeri
Juniperus conferta
Leymus arenarius
Limonium latifolium
Onopordum acanthium

Self-sown *Eryngium* seedlings will flower the following summer.

EUPHORBIA MYRSINITES
With its trailing stems of blue-green leaves, this plant adds form and color all through the year. The lime green flowers in spring are a brilliant contrast.

Helianthemum apenninum starts to open its papery white flowers in early summer. Regular deadheading helps prolong its season.

LOOKING AFTER THE SOIL

HOW WELL YOU TREAT YOUR SOIL may be the deciding factor in whether plants survive in times of drought. Although soils vary in their ability to retain moisture, there are scarcely any that do not benefit from generous additions of organic matter. On fast-draining soil, it provides a plant's lifeline.

ASSESSING YOUR SOIL TYPE

To understand how readily your soil might be affected by drought, you need to establish its type. Sandy soil, with fast-draining large particles, dries out quickly. It feels gritty when rubbed, is often light in color, and the grains will not stick together or form a ball. Thin, alkaline soil is almost as drought-prone. Often a pale grayish color, especially when dry, it usually consists of a shallow band over limestone, and the surface can be quite sticky when wet. Clay soil, composed of fine, closely packed particles, retains water longer but becomes bricklike and unworkable when dry, with surface cracks appearing. When moist, it retains its shape if squeezed and feels slightly greasy. A cold soil, it is slow to warm up in spring.

PREVENTING COMPACTION

Compacted soil damages plant growth. It is unlikely to be a problem if you mulch and add organic matter on a regular basis.

SURFACE CAPPING
Walking on damp soil or overwatering can cause a hard surface crust, or "cap," to form, preventing water (and oxygen) from reaching plant roots. Break up a cap if it occurs, but try never to walk on wet ground (if unavoidable, lay a board on the soil).

IMPERMEABLE LAYERS
Severe compaction creates a "hardpan," or almost impermeable layer, under the surface; water cannot drain and roots get waterlogged. Break it up and add lots of organic matter.

WAYS OF IMPROVING MOISTURE RETENTION

Adding organic matter is the best way to improve water retention. Worked in among the soil particles, it acts like a sponge, holding on to moisture and making it available to plants when rainfall is low. On heavy clay, incorporate coarse sand as well as organic matter to open up the soil and prevent cracking; it bakes hard in hot, dry conditions, damaging plant roots in the process. Dig in organic matter in autumn to give it time to break down into a crumb structure by the growing season.

NATURE'S WAY
Organic matter is naturally taken down into the soil by worms and beneficial microorganisms, which break it up into an excellent soil conditioner. Avoid excessive neatness in the garden, and some of the work will be done for you.

THE BEST ADDITIVES

There are many forms of organic matter, some better suited to different types of soil. As a guideline, you will need to apply a layer at least 2in (5cm) deep to gain any real improvement. Add more to sandy soil and, for maximum effect, dig it in while it is damp. Recycling garden waste into compost makes one of the cheapest soil conditioners, and you can make leafmold by stacking fallen leaves in a chicken-wire enclosure to decompose. Many local authorities also now offer good, weed-free compost, recycled from municipal waste. Always compost fresh animal manure until it is well rotted.

ANIMAL MANURE
When well rotted it is a source of organic matter and some nutrients.

MUSHROOM COMPOST
Contains lime; do not use on alkaline soil or acid-loving plants.

COMPOST
Wait until the texture turns crumbly. It is a source of organic matter and nutrients.

LEAFMOLD
Good conditioner with a low level of nutrients. Good for acid-loving plants.

MAKING COMPOST

Build up layers of soft, leafy material, such as grass clippings, spent foliage, and kitchen vegetable waste, and material such as tougher chopped prunings and straw. Bins can be of wood or plastic. If you have space, two bins are extremely useful so that you can add material to one while the other heap is rotting. Never apply compost to soil before the material is well rotted – brown, crumbly, and sweet-smelling. This usually takes about three months but can take a year or more. Chop up coarse material (prunings and tough stalks) and mix with the soft material (see above) to speed decompostion. The process is also greatly speeded by adding soil, fresh manure, or a commercial activator at intervals. Cover with a piece of old carpet to keep the heat in, then a lid. The heat created by the rotting process further fuels decomposition but is rarely high enough to kill weed seeds, so put only leafy growth on the pile. Never add diseased plants (or meat, which can attract vermin).

BUILDING UP THE LAYERS
Add the material by spreading it in layers. Avoid thick wads of grass clippings, which inhibit air flow. As the bin begins to fill, turn the contents to ensure an even breakdown.

THE IMPORTANCE OF MULCHING

MULCHES PLAY A VARIETY OF ROLES. They are essential in combating drought because they substantially reduce the amount of water lost from the soil by evaporation. They also suppress weeds, can look decorative, and, as they get broken down, organic mulches will gradually improve the soil.

NATURAL MULCHES

Organic mulches such as bark chips, rotted manure, and cocoa shells rot with time and generally need replacing at least every year. The rate at which they disappear depends on source, age, and particle size. Spread them at least 2in (5cm) deep onto moist ground. If possible, use materials with a large particle size; small, crumbly mulches, though good at conserving moisture, make a first-rate seedbed for weeds. Most organic mulches are ideally suited to shady areas. Gravel looks perfect in open, sunny gardens and is a natural companion for plants that thrive in these conditions.

BARK CHIPS
Variable in quality and particle size. Be sure to buy bark, not chipped wood.

GRAVEL
Excellent, long-lasting inorganic mulch, available in a range of colors and sizes.

GRASS CLIPPINGS
Compost with other material first. Never use grass freshly treated with herbicide.

COCOA SHELLS
A good light and porous mulch, with small amounts of nutrients.

SHEET MULCHES

Used on their own, unprepossessing sheet mulches are usually reserved for hidden vegetable patches or steep slopes. But, combined with a layer of gravel or bark chips (*see right*), they make a highly efficient mulch for the ornamental garden. There are two basic categories: nonporous types such as black plastic, which provide cover but, unless perforated, do not allow rainfall or air to penetrate, and porous fiber fleeces, including geotextiles. These let in water and oxygen but at the same time suppress weeds. They are extremely durable but, once in place, they make it almost impossible to add organic matter or fertilizers to the soil.

MATERIAL OPTIONS

Bonded fiber fleece Specifically made for mulching, long lasting and easy to lay. Allows water and air to pass through.

Woven geotextile One of the most expensive, but available in heavier gauges than fiber fleece. Extremely long lasting and hard wearing; good under pathways.

Black plastic Cheap and useful on well-drained, very sandy or gravelly soils that need to retain maximum moisture.

Newspaper Can be quite effective if several layers are used and thoroughly soaked after laying. Usually lasts for one season.

Old carpet Cheap and effective for small areas but will eventually rot.

LAYING ORGANIC MULCHES

Before laying a mulch, remove all perennial weeds then cultivate the ground. After about 10 days, hoe off any weeds that have germinated. Mulches are usually best laid in spring while the soil is still damp but has just started to warm up. Lightweight materials such as fine bark and cocoa shells are best applied on calm days, or wind may blow away the particles. These mulches are also best watered immediately afterward – water releases a gum in cocoa shells that binds the pieces together. If there are nearby paths or lawns, make a raised edge or curb to stop the mulch from constantly spilling over.

THE BEAUTY OF BARK
Bark chips, laid 2–6in (10–15cm) deep, are ideal, since their coarse texture allows rain through without making them cake together.

CONCEALING SHEET MULCHES

Sheet mulches must be laid before you begin planting but after the soil has been thoroughly prepared. After rolling out the sheeting, anchor it in position with plastic or wire pegs, or push the edges of the sheet into the ground with a spade. Put in the plants before spreading the decorative mulch. Make it at least 2in (5cm) deep, or the sheet may show through. If using gravel on large areas, you can add interest by varying the size of the gravel and including one or two larger rocks.

1 To plant, cut a crosswise slit in the sheet mulch and fold back the four corners. Make a suitably sized hole for the plant's rootball. Put in the plant and water in well, then fold the sheet mulch back in place.

2 Spread bark chips – or other ornamental mulch – over the sheet, brushing it under leaves and around plant stems with your hands. Make sure that the whole area is well and evenly covered.

BRIGHT ALTERNATIVES
Glass nuggets add lively color in dreary seasons. Use in small quantity and choose plant partners carefully for a cohesive, not chaotic, effect.

GOOD GARDEN SURFACES

THE WATER-WISE GARDEN OFFERS enormous scope for using surfaces other than lawn. Paving, cobblestones, gravel, or decking can be combined in imaginative ways that conserve moisture at the same time. These materials keep evaporation to a minimum, need little maintenance, and provide a cool root run for plants. A subtle mix of textures and colors can look good even in a tiny garden.

ON THE GARDEN FLOOR

Gravel is one of the most versatile materials, ideal as a mulch and background for plants (*see p.18*) but also suitable for more open spaces such as sitting areas. It needs to be laid on top of a firm subsoil base and layer of crushed stone, to barely more than 1in (2.5cm) deep so that you can walk on it comfortably rather than wade through. Gravel often looks best – and is easiest laid – given a neighboring hard surface or edge of cobblestones, paving slabs, bricks, or pavers. In any case, do not lay it right up to the house entrance, since it is easily tracked indoors. When laying paving, bed bricks or slabs on sand with just a few held in place with cement, so that rain drains through. Where a harsh climate necessitates sparse planting, tiles or glass blocks can introduce small areas of contrast. Whatever the material, choose colors and textures that blend with the house.

▶ DESIGN IN THE ROUND
Cobblestones and gravel are easily worked into curving shapes and naturally complement one another as well as the plants.

◀ STONE AND GLASS
Glass blocks (far left) create clear pools of color among rough-textured gravel but are not meant for areas of hard wear and tear. More durable concrete rounds (left) are reminiscent of a log path but are good in a dry garden, where shades of gray predominate instead of woodland green and brown.

DECKING BY DESIGN

Wooden decking has a pleasantly flexible feel to walk on and also allows rain to pass through to plant roots below. You can use a natural shade of preservative or introduce color. Although decking can be set at the same level as the rest of the garden, it often looks better slightly raised, but supporting structures must be strong enough to take the weight. If cobblestones or gravel are used as a surrounding, you can create the illusion of a jetty over a dry riverbed.

MAKING IT SAFE

• Ridged (grooved) lumber helps prevent slipping when the surface is wet. If algae forms, remove it with a fungicide and stiff broom. Special deck paints for boats, which create a nonslip, gritty surface, can also be used.
• Use pressure-treated lumber and supplement with a preservative. Do not allow joists to come into contact with soil.
• Put handrails at the side of any steps.

HARMONIOUS WOOD
Decking provides a sympathetic link between garden and home. Boards can create bold directional lines and angles, while prefab panels come in a variety of patterns and are easily laid on level ground.

DECKING PANELS

PLANTING IN PAVING

Take the edge off of hard-surface areas by filling the cracks between paving stones with creeping plants, such as thyme. Even in dry climates, there is usually sufficient moisture beneath the slabs for the efficient root systems of alpines to exploit this zone. The effect is enhanced when the occasional slab is left out and a taller or bushier plant allowed to fill up the space.

PAVING INTERPLANTED WITH THYME

EFFECTIVE GROUNDCOVERS

ONE OF THE CHALLENGES in drought-resistant gardening is the creation of interesting plant combinations that require little maintenance yet provide efficient groundcover (if necessary, the plant roots helping to bind the soil). In many dry gardens, planting is sparse and concentrates on the bold use of key specimens. The art of good groundcover, however, lies in creating drifts of plants that are broken by an occasional change in height, shape, and color.

GETTING THE BEST RESULTS FROM PLANTS

The gray foliage of many drought-resistant plants acts as the perfect foil for darker leaf or flower colors, particularly purple. Aim for the bulk of the plants you choose to grow no more than 12–18in (30–45cm) tall. At this height they are unlikely to be damaged by wind. Choose plants with a spreading or hummocky habit, including a proportion of evergreens such as *Santolina*, lavenders, junipers, and sage so that there is some cover and color in winter, and arrange them in unevenly shaped drifts. Then, as they grow into each other, they will achieve a pleasing informality. At the same time, they will create a slightly undulating framework in which small gaps should be left for more upright or spiky plants – the accent plants, with strong foliage or striking color.

PLANTING TIPS

• Incorporate as much organic matter (such as compost) as possible after clearing the ground of weeds, especially perennial weeds.
• Plant in autumn to give plants a chance to establish before the dry season.
• Small, young plants establish more quickly in dry conditions than older, larger plants.
• Remove any leggy shoots to encourage the development of bushy, sturdy plants.
• Plants with roots to bind soil include *Atriplex, Elymus, Epimedium, Eragrostis, Helianthemum, Rosa rugosa,* and thyme.

TAPESTRY OF PLANTS
Mounds of purple sage, lavender, and thyme are punctuated by spires of Verbascum, *orange splashes of poppy, and grassy leaves of sedge.*

GOOD GROUNDCOVER PLANTS

LOW-GROWING	MEDIUM HEIGHT	TALL PLANTS
Herbaceous and rock plants	**Herbaceous and rock plants**	**Herbaceous plants**
Acaena, Alyssum, Antennaria, Arabis, Aubrieta, Cerastium, Epimedium, Saponaria, Sedum, thyme	*Artemisia, Nepeta* such as *N. × faassenii, Origanum, Pachysandra, Phlomis russeliana, Salvia* such as *S. × superba, Senecio, Stachys*	*Acanthus, Achillea* 'Coronation Gold', *Anaphalis margaritacea, Gaillardia*
Shrubby plants	**Shrubby plants**	**Shrubby plants**
Cotoneaster horizontalis, Hedera (ivy), *Helianthemum, Hypericum calycinum, Juniperus conferta*	*Artemisia, Genista, Salvia officinalis* (sage), *Santolina*	*Atriplex halimus, Elaeagnus angustifolia,* lavender, *Perovskia,* rosemary, *Rosa rugosa, Ruta graveolens* (rue)
Ornamental grasses	**Ornamental grasses**	**Ornamental grasses**
Briza, Festuca (fescue), *Holcus*	*Elymus, Helictotrichon, Koeleria, Stipa*	*Eragrostis, Leymus, Melica, Pennisetum*

▲ *For details of hardiness, see Good Plants for Dry Places, starting on p.47.*

LOOKING AT LAWNS

No traditional lawngrass mixture can survive drought and yet remain green if closely mown. Normally, the main reason for rapid browning is mowing too closely – shaving off the plants' "food factory." Well-established lawns of suitable species can completely brown off in summer and then turn green again when moisture returns.

During periods of moisture, mow grass shorter than during times of drought, and keep the mower blades sharp. If the grass starts to brown, raise the height of cut to give only a light trim. When sowing lawn seed or sodding a lawn, try to use a high proportion of species and selections that are able to tolerate the given conditions, including soil type and light levels, as well as available moisture. Also consider whether the lawn will be required to tolerate heavy or light foot traffic and whether you are prepared to provide water, fertilizer, and pesticides if necessary. As an alternative, on sandy soil you could make a small lawn of prostrate thyme (*see T. serpyllum, p.67*).

THYME IS RIGHT
A thyme lawn doubles as a sundial. Prostrate thymes can withstand being walked on; it heightens the aroma from their creeping stems.

WHICH GRASS TO CHOOSE

Lawn grasses are split into cool-season for temperate areas (preferring 60–75°F/15–25°C) and warm-season for subtropical climates (preferring 75–95°F/26–35°C).

COOL-SEASON GRASSES

Bluegrass, slender red fescue; hard fescue; smooth-stalked meadow grass; and, for very dry conditions where a fine finish is not needed, crested wheatgrass (*Agropyron cristatum*) and Western wheatgrass (*Agropyron smithii*).

WARM-SEASON GRASSES

Bermuda grass (*Cynodon dactylon*); *Zoysia*; St. Augustine grass (*Stenotaphrum secundatum*)

CHOOSING THE RIGHT PLANTS

A GROWING ENVIRONMENTAL AWARENESS and appreciation of native landscapes, especially where they are under threat, is changing attitudes and encouraging gardeners to take a much more natural approach. Plants such as grasses are now highly valued for their easy charm, grace, and ability to grow well without undue amounts of coddling. Match plant with site and gardening becomes liberating not restricting, and the effects created are satisfying in every sense.

NATURAL SURVIVORS

For the best drought-resistant plants look at what grows well in the wild in comparable habitats and conditions – for example desert plants, prairie plants, seashore natives, and Mediterranean shrubs and bulbs. Many have developed easily identifiable characteristics (*see p.32*) and often make excellent natural partners. Garden designers are drawing on this to produce combinations worth considering. Often called "new-style" perennial plantings (*see the plan on the next page*), these use plants, appropriate to the conditions, that need no staking or winter protection. Once established, such plantings need minimal care.

LIFE ON THE EDGE *Tucked between rocks on a sandy shore, thrift (Armeria) manages to survive on the meager amounts of moisture held in the crevices. Other plants such as Tamarix, Crambe, and Eryngium maritimum (sea holly), which have little but sand to draw water from and are buffeted by salt-laden winds, are real drought survivors.*

◄ EASY-CARE PLANTS Allium, *yellow asphodel, and a red* Euphorbia *provide layers of color and shape.*

NEW-STYLE PERENNIAL BORDER

Try to make the arrangement look as natural as possible – loose drifts help produce a continuous flow of interest. *Allium* may slowly diminish, but they self-seed, and it is easy to add more bulbs if needed. The *Euphorbia*'s spent flower stems are best cut back, and deadheading the *Nepeta* will encourage many more blooms, but leave the dried heads of *Achillea*, *Allium*, and grasses for autumn and winter display. Here, the garden is seen in midsummer.

The large, flat, dark red flowerheads of *Achillea millefolium* 'Sammetriese' start to open in midsummer and are extremely long-lasting.

Nepeta × *faassenii* makes a grayish mound of aromatic foliage, covered from mid-summer with a succession of lavender-blue flowers.

ECHINOPS RITRO
The round flower globes, which appear in late summer, echo the shape of the Allium *on a smaller scale. They are excellent for attracting bees and butterflies.*

MORE CHOICES

FLOWERING PLANTS

Anthemis
Asclepias tuberosa
Dictamnus albus
Gaillardia
Gypsophila repens
Lychnis flos-jovis
Phlomis russeliana
Salvia sclarea
Sedum
Verbascum

GOOD GRASSES

Cortaderia selloana
Elymus magellanicus
Eragrostis curvula
Melica altissima

Over summer, the evergreen leaves of *Stipa arundinacea* gradually turn tawny, until in winter they are entirely russet-brown. A decorative plant all year.

PLANTING PLAN

1 3 *Achillea millefolium* 'Sammetriese', 24in/60cm apart
2 3 *Echinops ritro*, 24in/60cm apart
3 1 *Stipa arundinacea*
4 3 *Origanum laevigatum*, 18in/45cm apart
5 3 *Echinacea purpurea* 'Robert Bloom', 24in/60cm apart
6 3 *Nepeta* × *faassenii*, 18in/45cm apart
7 3 *Helictotrichon sempervirens*, 12in/30cm apart
8 3 *Euphorbia griffithii*, 24in/60cm apart
9 4 *Asphodeline lutea*, 12in/30cm apart (small plants)
10 9 *Allium cristophii*, arranged informally

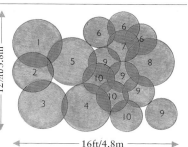

12½ft/3.8m

16ft/4.8m

Helictotrichon sempervirens
has leaves in an eye-catching
shade of blue-gray; tall,
slender flowering stems are
produced in summer.

ECHINACEA PURPUREA
The red-purple flowers of
'Robert Bloom', with their
high-domed rusty cones,
provide useful color in late
summer and autumn.

The flowerheads of
Euphorbia griffithii are an
unusual dusky orange-red
that harmonizes well with
other plants. It spreads by
underground runners.

Fat seedcases decorate the
stems of Asphodeline lutea
after the yellow starry
flowers have gone.

The spherical flowers of
Allium cristophii have impact
even in autumn, long after
they have faded and
turned brown.

Origanum laevigatum bears
its flowers on wiry stems
from late spring to autumn.

WHICH PLANTS CAN COPE?

Plants from naturally dry regions have all evolved a strategy of one kind or another for surviving drought. Many have developed distinctive types of foliage (*see opposite*), often pleasing to the eye and easy to use in a decorative way. Roots, too, must be capable of seeking out every drop of water. Those plants that have adapted best to the dry life are known as xerophytes, and drought-resistant gardening is sometimes called xeriscaping.

FOLIAGE SURVIVAL TECHNIQUES

Generally, the smaller a plant's leaf the more likely it is to be able to withstand drought, because little water is lost from the surface. Some grasses can roll their blades inward, making them even narrower. In plants such as broom, many or even all leaves have been lost, with stems taking over most of the job of photosynthesis.

Gray foliage is another characteristic. Light-colored leaves reflect glare. Sometimes the grayness or silveriness is caused by a covering of hairs; these help lower the temperature within the leaf, reducing moisture loss, and also limit the drying effects of wind. Glaucous foliage, such as that of eucalyptus, often gets its bluish tone from a waxy coating. Other leaves are protected by a leathery skin. Many plants combine techniques: for instance, the fleshy leaves of succulents, such as *Sedum*, not only store water but also have a waxy surface.

UNDERGROUND SOLUTIONS

Many desert plants have developed long, deep taproots to search for water at lower, cooler levels. Plants in shallow soil, especially over rock, produce fine, fibrous, very extensive root systems that can seek out water between each and every particle. Where drought is seasonal, bulbs and corms produce foliage and flowers in the cooler, moister times of year. In the dry season they go dormant, storing food underground to provide energy for new growth when the rains return.

The yucca's spiny leaf tips repel animals in search of foliage to eat

Upright leaves suffer less from intense sunlight

Leaves have an extra-tough skin

Taproot can store moisture and food

The root will fork or form side roots if it encounters a stone or other obstacle

In loose-particled soil, such as sandy soil, there is nothing to hinder a probing root

A YUCCA EXPOSED
This young yucca has quickly developed a long taproot capable of plumbing the depths. Its leaves have a tough, waxy skin that retains moisture and can withstand extremes of heat.

FOLIAGE THAT CAN WITHSTAND DROUGHT

Eucalyptus perriniana
This gum tree is not wilting. Instead, it has naturally drooping leaves that turn away from the sun in order to reduce the effect of its rays and mimimize water loss. (*See also p.48.*)

Sedum spathulifolium 'Purpureum'
A tiny succulent with several tactics. It can store water in its fleshy leaves; tightly clustered, they present only a small surface area to the sun and efficiently collect any moisture.

Portulaca oleracea
Known as purslane, this is cultivated in Mediterranean countries for its water-retentive, fleshy leaves, which give a refreshing bite to salads. It has some brightly colored relatives for the flower border (*see p.69*).

Eryngium maritimum
The leaves of this seashore dweller have an extremely tough, leathery skin that inhibits moisture loss. It also has a long taproot that travels deep to find water in impoverished sandy soil (*see also p.60*).

Sempervivum ciliosum
A rock plant that combines strategies. The leaves curve inward and are covered in sun-reflecting hairs (*cilium* means hair). It often grows among rocks to protect it from heat. (*See also p.67.*)

Senecio cineraria 'Cirrus'
A thick coating of fine hairs gives this plant its gray, felty appearance. Hairs often create an attractive silky or furry look but also make the plants susceptible to winter cold and moisture.

Festuca ovina
The blue-green grassy quills have a very small surface area, losing very little water. The roots form a fine, fibrous mass, maximizing the number of root hairs that can draw moisture from the soil.

Pinus thunbergii
Pines are among the most drought-resistant conifers. The needles have not only a small surface area but also a thick, waxy skin that helps seal in moisture and prevent them from drying out in wind. (*Other pines, see p.49.*)

PLANTS FOR DIFFICULT PLACES

AS WELL AS ADAPTING TO DROUGHT, plants in some sites have further problems to deal with. Dry shade under trees, especially evergreens, creates particular difficulties, often in gardens that are otherwise relatively damp. In coastal sites plants must withstand exposure to salt and wind, and in real desert, where annual rainfall is less than 10in/25cm, survive exceptional extremes of heat and cold.

DEALING WITH DRY SHADE

The combination of poor light, impoverished soil, and tree or shrub roots makes dry shade one of the most limiting environments. Removing trees' lowest branches to let in light and improve air circulation encourages better plant growth. Spring-flowering bulbs that go dormant during the driest period are usually a good choice for such a site.

LAMIUM MACULATUM

PLANTS FOR DRY SHADE

HERBACEOUS PERENNIALS
Bergenia, Brunnera, Cortaderia selloana (pampas grass), *Epimedium*, Lamium*, Pachysandra*, Pulmonaria, Waldsteinia**

BULBS AND CORMS
Allium, Anemone blanda, Cyclamen coum and *C. hederifolium, Eranthis hyemalis*

SHRUBS
Cotoneaster horizontalis, Euonymus, Hedera (ivy)*, *Ilex* (holly), *Prunus laurocerasus* (cherry laurel), *Ribes* (flowering currant), *Ruscus* (butcher's broom)*, *Santolina, Symphoricarpos, Vinca minor* (periwinkle)*
*makes a good groundcover
Dry shade plants are often unsuitable for sun.

BY THE SEA

Fast-draining sandy soil and strong drying winds are a real problem in coastal gardens. Hedges of salt-resistant trees and shrubs help shield other plants. When choosing garden plants, look at what grows wild along the shore for a useful guide. Seaside natives withstand drought because they have developed a physiology that keeps out sea water. A plant name ending in *maritima* or *maritimum* is also a good indication.

GOOD PLANTS FOR COASTAL SITES

FLOWERING PERENNIALS
Armeria (thrift), *Cortaderia* (pampas grass), *Crambe, Eryngium, Kniphofia* (red-hot poker), *Limonium* (sea lavender), *Oenothera*

FLOWERING SHRUBS
Cistus, Cytisus (broom), fuchsias, *Genista,* x *Halimiocistus, Hebe*, hydrangeas, *Olearia, Romneya coulteri*, rosemary, *Spartium*

SEASIDE HEDGING PLANTS
Baccharis halimifolia, Crataegus (hawthorn), x *Cupressocyparis leylandii* (Leyland cypress), *Elaeagnus* (evergreen types), *Escallonia, Fuchsia* 'Riccartoni', *Griselinia littoralis, Hippophae rhamnoides, Olearia* x *haastii, Pyracantha, Rosa rugosa, Tamarix* (tamarisk)

INTO THE DESERT

The arid areas of the world produce the most dramatic, sometimes bizarre, of all plant adaptations for storing water or minimizing its loss. A desert dweller such as the saguaro cactus can store up to eight tons of water in the reservoirs of its thorny, towering columns. Many xerophytes have vicious spines – added protection against grazing animals. Plants such as *Parkinsonia* (*see p.49*) may resort to shedding leaves (though this can happen, too, in temperate climates). The ocotillo (*Fouquieria splendens*) keeps its leaves for a few weeks only before returning to being a bundle of thorny stems. The wide spacing between desert plants is no accident, since it prevents competition for water reserves. In some deserts, four-fifths of some plants lies beneath the ground, the roots tapping into moisture stored up to 100ft/30m down.

▲ SPIKES AND BOULDERS
The juxtaposition of shapes is one of the most important elements in arid landscape gardens. Carefully placed rocks surround this Agave.

▼ THE DESERT GARDEN
Flowering may be brief, but for architectural form, few plants compare with desert natives (see plan on next page for a desert garden).

A DESERT GARDEN

If you can give them the right conditions, desert plants present the opportunity to combine some of the most arresting, architectural shapes in the plant kingdom. As in a natural arid landscape, rocks and boulders are an important element. Many of the plants are tender (*see pp.47–69*), but a similar style could be created in a cold climate if the plants were plunged in pots for summer, then lifted and protected under cover in winter.

PLANTING PLAN

1 3 *Yucca whipplei*, 30in/75cm apart
2 3 *Lampranthus haworthii*, 12in/30cm apart
3 1 *Lantana montevidensis*
4 1 *Aloe ferox*
5 1 *Opuntia robusta*
6 1 *Echinocactus grusonii*
7 2 *Atriplex halimus*, 24in/60cm apart

11½ft/3.5m

16ft/5m

The slender, finely toothed leaves of *Yucca whipplei* slowly grow to nearly 3ft/1m. Plants die once they have set seed but usually take many years to produce their summer spikes of fragrant, creamy bells.

LAMPRANTHUS HAWORTHII
A succulent plant that trails over the ground, its gray-green, fleshy foliage studded with eye-catching, purplish pink daisy flowers.

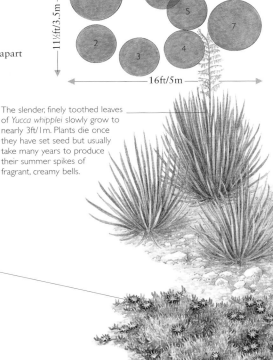

Heads of pale to deep violet flowers decorate *Lantana montevidensis* during summer, standing up well above the leaves. The slender stems of this spreading shrub will form a dense mat.

ECHINOCACTUS GRUSONII Often called the golden barrel cactus, the spiny, ribbed spheres very slowly become more elongated in shape. They are decorated with rings of yellow flowers in summer.

CONSERVATION ALERT

Many of the world's plant species, including many cacti and other succulents, are under threat of extinction in the wild because of habitat destruction and overcollection. Gardeners can help with the preservation of endangered species:

• Be aware that many plants, especially cacti, require at least several years to reach landscape size and are therefore economically unfeasible to produce. Large specimens of such plants offered for sale, especially if they are offered at low prices, have almost certainly been wild collected. Unless the supplier can prove that plants have been nursery raised (usually from seed) or legally rescued, refuse to buy them.

• Participate in plant-rescue operations, then grow the plants in your own garden or arrange to give them to a botanic garden.

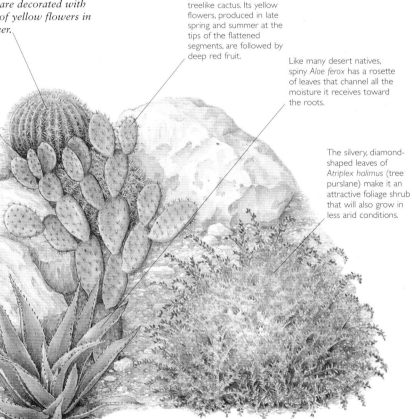

Opuntia robusta (prickly pear) is a shrubby or treelike cactus. Its yellow flowers, produced in late spring and summer at the tips of the flattened segments, are followed by deep red fruit.

Like many desert natives, spiny *Aloe ferox* has a rosette of leaves that channel all the moisture it receives toward the roots.

The silvery, diamond-shaped leaves of *Atriplex halimus* (tree purslane) make it an attractive foliage shrub that will also grow in less arid conditions.

MAKING THE BEST USE OF WATER

Plants in containers inevitably need regular watering, but by choosing the most suitable plants (*see plan overleaf*), containers, and soil mix, (*see p.42*) you can reduce the amount required. Similarly, some methods of watering the garden are more efficient than others (*see p.44*). Plants may need to rely on stored rainwater in spells of drought and during watering bans. Then, it may also be necessary to recycle waste domestic, or "gray," water (*see p.45*).

GARDENING IN CONTAINERS

Many drought-resistant plants are suited to life in a container, since they can tolerate a degree of neglect. Some of the most exciting are also the least hardy, but containers give cold-climate gardeners the chance to grow them, provided plants can be protected in a greenhouse or conservatory in winter. Water-retaining crystals and non-porous containers (*see p.42*) reduce the amount of watering needed, as do all kinds of mulches (*see p.22 and below*).

FALLEN BOUNTY
Pine cones, gathered from the forest floor, make an unusual but natural-looking mulch. Match cone size with the size of the pot.

INSPIRED BY THE SEA
Combined with the right plant, a mulch of shells, pebbles, and sparkling glass nuggets will help conserve moisture in the soil mix.

◀ TWO OF A KIND Cordyline *and* Agave *are good partners for each other and for flowering plants.*

A Container Garden

A group of containers of varying shapes and heights perfectly displays foliage textures and forms. Some of these plants (shown here in late summer) will need winter protection in cold climates. Brilliant *Gazania* flowers circle the upright purple spears of a *Cordyline,* and a *Sedum* and *Convolvulus cneorum* trail naturally over the sides of their pots, as do the mats of foliage formed by the neat rosettes of two *Sempervivum.*

PLANTING PLAN

1 2 *Sedum* 'Ruby Glow', planted close to pot edges
2 1 *Hebe* 'Red Edge'
3 3 *Sempervivum montanum*
4 2 *Agapanthus* 'Blue Moon'
5 1 *Cordyline* 'Purple Tower'
6 3 *Gazania* Harlequin Hybrids
7 2 *Convolvulus cneorum*
8 3 *Sempervivum giuseppii*

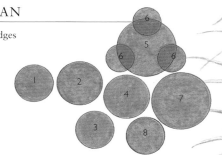

One of the lower-growing *Agapanthus,* 'Blue Moon' is ideal for a pot. It must be moved into some sort of winter protection in cold regions once the foliage has died down.

Sedum 'Ruby Glow'.
This small Sedum has a naturally sprawling habit and does well in a container, where its flowers spill over the sides.

With its purple-tinged young leaves, *Hebe* 'Red Edge' is a handsome shrub even without its lilac flowers. These open in mid-summer and gradually fade to white. It will need winter protection in most areas.

Rosettes of *Sempervivum montanum* multiply to cover a shallow pot. Occasional thick red flower spikes shoot up from their centers in summer.

Cordyline australis 'Purple Tower' adds architectural focus. In cold climates it needs the protection of a greenhouse or conservatory in winter.

MORE CHOICES

GOOD FOLIAGE

Aloe ferox, Cotoneaster horizontalis, Festuca glauca, Helichrysum petiolare, Lotus hirsutus, Opuntia robusta, Pennisetum alopecuroides, Phormium tenax, Yucca filamentosa

ATTRACTIVE FLOWERS

Brachyscome iberidifolia, Dimorphotheca pluvialis, × *Halimiocistus wintonensis* 'Merrist Wood Cream', *Halimium* 'Susan', *Lampranthus haworthii, Nerium oleander, Phlomis fruticosa, Portulaca grandiflora, Saponaria*

AROMATIC PLANTS

Lavender, oregano, rosemary, *Salvia sclarea*, thyme

Eye-catching *Gazania* flowers are produced all summer but, like several African daisies, open only in sun. Best grown as an annual in temperate climates, it also makes a good seaside plant. Available in a wide range of colors.

CONVOLVULUS CNEORUM
A shrub that revels in sun. Its main flowering period is from late spring to midsummer, but it often produces an occasional fluted trumpet later in the season.

The tight, rounded rosettes of vigorous *Sempervivum giuseppii* are flushed dark red at the tips.

WATERING CONTAINERS

MANY OF THE SAME rules apply to watering containers as to watering the garden (*see p.44*). Water well at planting, settling soil mix by using a fine rose on the can. Then, water thoroughly but only when plants need it, at the coolest times of day (water soil mix, not foliage). Use mulches, and even though you are trying to conserve moisture, ensure containers have good drainage holes.

CHOOSING THE BEST CONTAINERS

Terracotta sets off plants to advantage but, since it is porous, soil mix dries out fast. Paint or seal pots inside with varnish, or line with plastic punctured with drainage holes. Plastic and fiberglass pots retain moisture well but can get hot in the sun. Standing them inside another container, such as a wooden planter, helps insulate plant roots from the heat. Reconstituted stone keeps roots cool in hot spots. The larger the volume of soil mix, the slower it dries out, so choose big containers when possible. If you group pots, they protect one another from heat and drying wind.

PERFECT FINISH
Glazed ceramic pots are a good choice and come in lovely colors. They need drainage holes and must be frostproof in cold climates.

SOIL MIXES

Multipurpose soil mixes based on peat dry out fast and are difficult to remoisten. If choosing a peat substitute-based mix, opt for a moisture-retentive material such as coir. As well as adding crystals (*below*), incorporate some fine sand to aid rapid saturation when watering. Soil-based mixes are slower to dry out. Leave plenty of space for watering between soil mix and pot rim, and catch excess in a tray (replacing it with raised blocks in winter for good drainage).

ADDING WATER-RETAINING CRYSTALS
Specially formulated crystals swell with water and act as micro-reservoirs, slowly releasing moisture into the soil mix. Add before planting, and use only the amount recommended.

WATERING IN WINTER

Container plants, especially evergreens, may sometimes need watering in winter. Wind has a very drying effect. Keep a check and water in mild spells only, never to frozen soil.

IRRIGATION SYSTEMS FOR CONTAINERS

Automatic and semi-automatic irrigation systems can deliver water efficiently to a group of containers – straight to the soil mix and the plants' roots – as well as saving time. It is usually better to put together a system to suit your own needs rather than buy a standard multipurpose kit. A dripper, or drip-head, is used to supply each container. Each dripper is fitted to a small-diameter, flexible pipe (the microtube), which in turn fits into a larger supply pipe connected to an outside faucet. Simple push-on plastic fixtures are used to make the connections, and adaptors and elbow connectors aid installation and help in running the supply pipe around corners.

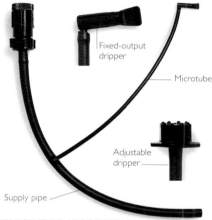

Fixed-output dripper

Microtube

Adjustable dripper

Supply pipe

WHICH TYPE OF DRIPPER?
Fixed-output drippers trickle out the water at a predetermined rate. Where plants need differing amounts of water, choose adjustable drippers so that you can vary the flow.

INSTALLING THE SYSTEM

• Cut the supply pipe to length once you have arranged your containers, and connect the microtubes to it at suitable intervals. Most systems include a punch for puncturing the correct size hole in the supply pipe. Put a stop-plug in the end.

• Large pots (especially if they contain a collection of plants) often need two or more drippers to ensure even watering. To decide the number of drippers, measure how much water each container requires using a watering can (*see below left*) and the amount each dripper delivers (sometimes given in the manufacturer's instructions). If necessary, add in extra drippers when you have seen how the system is operating.

• Check regularly that the system is delivering water efficiently, and clean the nozzles when necessary since they are liable to become clogged with soil mix.

FULLY AUTOMATIC SYSTEMS

Computerized automatic systems are expensive but make it possible to turn on the water at any time (including when you're asleep or away from home). The most sophisticated employ sensors to ascertain soil-moisture levels, but for a container garden it is better to work out the individual requirements of each container according to its size and use an automatic timer in conjunction with adjustable flow drippers. To set the timer, measure the amount of water needed daily by each container using a watering can, then measure the amount discharged by the dripper over a given time.

COMPUTERIZED TIMER   SIMPLE TIMER

TIMING THE FLOW
A computerized timer (above left) *releases water on a programmed setting; a simple timer* (right) *turns water off after a preset period.*

WATERING FOR MAXIMUM EFFICIENCY

FOR WATERING TO BE EFFECTIVE it needs to be given in the right quantity and at the right time of day, season, and the plant's own life cycle. Sprinklers are seldom the answer because they use a lot of water in an inefficient way, resulting in runoff and capping of the soil surface. Water thoroughly when needed; do not give small, frequent amounts, which encourages surface rooting.

GIVING PLANTS A GOOD START

The most important time to water is at planting and immediately after, especially when putting container-grown plants into open ground. Before planting, thoroughly wet the rootball by standing the plant, in its pot, in a bucket of water until the air bubbles stop rising. After planting, water in well, and in dry conditions continue to water for the next few weeks, especially in spring and summer. The plant should then be making new growth, including new roots. Ease off watering, or it will stifle root development and make the plant dependent on watering. Do not plant in hot, dry spells.

RESERVOIR EFFECT
A low, saucerlike depression around the plant, with the soil mounded into walls, acts like a reservoir and prevents water from running away, especially when planting on a slope.

RIGHT DIRECTION
By inserting a pipe at the side of the planting hole, water can be channeled toward deep soil, encouraging the roots to extend in the right direction in their search for moisture.

EFFECTIVE SYSTEMS

For borders and vegetable and fruit plots, perforated hoses (known as leaky pipes or soaker or seep hoses) are effective at delivering water accurately, straight to the soil and with a minimum of evaporation. Made of plastic or rubber that is designed to emit water either along the whole length or from tiny holes at short intervals, the hose is threaded among plants close to the ground surface. It is often a good idea to run the hose through a layer of mulch to avoid holes becoming clogged with soil.

▲ DRIP-FEED THE SOIL
Water oozes into the soil above plant roots along the entire length of a seep hose.

▶ MAKE USE OF A MULCH
Laying a perforated hose in a gravel mulch stops holes from becoming blocked.

WHEN TO WATER

In summer, water in early morning or evening, when evaporation rates are low and the water has a chance to soak into the soil. Some plants need more water at certain stages of their life cycle. Young ornamental trees are more likely to be damaged by a shortage of water in the first half of summer than in the second. Fruit trees should not go short while the fruits are swelling. This applies, too, to cane and bush fruit, and to vegetables such as potatoes, squash, and peas while their tubers or fruits are developing. Avoid waiting to water until plants actually wilt, especially vegetables, or irreversible damage may occur. Do not let tomato plants go short of water while in flower. It can cause blossom-end rot, which damages the fruit.

RECYCLING WATER

Rainwater is easily recycled by connecting a water tank or barrel to a downspout. Make use of garage and shed roofs as well as the house roof. If the water is covered and free from algae it will last for six months. A rainwater barrel can store 30–50 gallons/ 120–200 liters. Because of the weight of water, it must stand on a firm base. Volume can be increased by linking barrels with a short pipe inserted into the overflow sockets, or you can buy larger tanks. (Thoroughly clean any tank that has previously been used to store something else.) A small submersible pump connected to a hose boosts delivery to distant parts of the garden.

GRAY WATER

This is the term used for domestic water that has been used for washing dishes or bathing. Given that the average bath uses 30 gallons/ 120 liters, it can be well worth recycling.
• Store in a dedicated container, and don't mix with other water.
• Use as soon as possible after it has cooled.
• Bathwater is more suitable than used water from the kitchen.
• Do not use water containing bleach or strong detergent.
• Do not apply directly onto plant leaves, but water the adjacent soil or container soil mix.
• Try to rotate the types of water given to any one area, and avoid the persistent use of gray water on one patch of ground.
• Do not use with a dripper system to avoid clogging nozzles.

SAVING RAINWATER

The water you collect from your house roof alone could get you through a period of drought, provided you have allowed for enough storage. A barrel connected to a garage or shed roof will provide even more. Do not collect water from a new roof or one that has been recently retarred.

WATER BARREL

Downspout from gutter

Cover for safety and to keep water clean

Overflow pipe

Tap at level that allows watering can to fit beneath

Secure stand built of bricks or insulation blocks. Plastic stands are also available

GOOD PLANTS FOR DRY PLACES

THE FOLLOWING PLANTS can all cope with a scarcity of water. Most are adapted to life in the sun, but a few like shade. Tender plants from hot, dry climates can sometimes survive rather low temperatures but will not if there is excessive moisture. Symbols indicate each plant's preferred growing conditions.

▨ *Plant prefers full sun* ▨ *Plant prefers partial shade* ❋ *Plant tolerates full shade*
Hardiness zone ranges are given as **Zx–x**
Min. °F/°C *Indicates minimum temperature for tender plants*

GARDEN TREES

TREES PROVIDE SHADE and some, especially conifers, help lessen the drying effects of wind. Many of these trees will, if planted in groups with shrubs, make a shelterbelt. With shelter, the garden becomes a more pleasant place to sit and offers conditions where more vulnerable plants can thrive; this is particularly true in seaside areas where salt winds severely limit plant choice.

Acacia dealbata (Mimosa)
Evergreen tree with deliciously fragrant heads of small, fluffy, round, yellow flowers, borne at the branch tips from winter to early summer. The silvery, fernlike leaves resist moisture loss. Like many woody plants in the pea family, it resents hard pruning. Can be grown in marginal areas if given the shelter of a wall. Height varies, depending on growing conditions, from 16ft/5m to 100ft/30m.
▨ **Z9–10**

Arbutus (Strawberry tree)
Small genus of spreading, often shrublike evergreen

Fruits

Flowers

ARBUTUS UNEDO

trees with attractive reddish peeling bark. *A. unedo* produces small, white or pink, pitcher-shaped flowers in

autumn, its strawberry-like fruits not ripening until the following year. *A. andrachne* flowers in spring, with fruits ripening in autumn. Both reach up to 26ft/8m and can be grown on alkaline soil, unlike the much taller *A. menziesii*, which needs acidic conditions.
▨ **Z7–9**

Cedrus (Cedar)
Handsome conifers for gardens with plenty of space. Wind and drought-resistant, and roughly conical in shape, they can reach 130ft/40m high with a 33ft/10m spread. Cedars make imposing

◀ SPRING SHOW *Yellow* Tulipa tarda *complements the green flowerheads of* Euphorbia *in late spring.*

CORDYLINE AUSTRALIS
'VARIEGATA'

specimens on sweeping lawns or terraces. *C. libani* 'Sargentii' (Z7–9) is slower growing, with weeping branches, and more suitable for a small garden.

Cordyline australis
(New Zealand cabbage palm)
An architectural, palmlike tree, up to 33ft/10m tall. Long, arching green leaves may be variegated. Where not hardy, grow in a container (which will limit its height to 10ft/3m) and overwinter in a greenhouse or conservatory. The leaves of outdoor plants can be protected by wrapping as for *Phormium* (see p.62).
 Z10–11
C. australis, see p.38
'Purple Tower', *see p.41*

Crataegus (Hawthorn)
Thorny, mainly deciduous trees and shrubs, well able to survive in inhospitable sites, particularly as hedging. *C. laciniata* (Z6–8) is ideal for an exposed dry garden, especially by the sea. Leaves are glossy and deeply lobed;

clusters of white flowers in late spring and early summer develop into showy, red fruits in autumn. Makes a good specimen up to 26ft/8m tall.

Cupressus (Cypress)
Evergreen conifers that form a dense, bushy screen – ideal for windbreaks or tall hedges in mild seaside areas. *C. macrocarpa* (Z7–10) can reach 100ft/30m with a spread of 13ft/4m, increasing with age, or can be grown as a hedge. Its lemon-scented leaves are a somber dark green. *C. sempervirens* (Z8–10) makes the thin, 65ft-/20m-high spires that punctuate Mediterranean hillsides. 'Stricta', to 10ft/3m, is almost pencil thin and very effective in formal gardens.

Eucalyptus (Gum tree)
Wide range of species, mostly drought-tolerant and with aromatic, gray-green leaves, though juvenile and adult leaves may differ from each other in shape and color. With age, *E. gunnii* (Z8–10) develops a spreading shape

CRATAEGUS LACINIATA

and colorful peeling bark. Can be regularly pruned hard to restrict its size and retain its rounded, silver-blue juvenile leaves. *E. parvifolia* (to 50ft/15m) can be grown on shallow alkaline soil in Z9–10; *E. pauciflora* subsp. *niphophila* (Z8–10) makes a small tree (to 20ft/6m), its stems covered in white, waxy bloom. *E. perriniana* (Z9–10) also remains fairly small (13–33ft/4–10m), with long, drooping adult leaves.

E. perriniana, see p.33

Ilex aquifolium
(English holly)
Spiny-leaved, dense, evergreen small tree or shrub, good in hedging or when grown as a specimen. Separate male and female plants, with only females producing the bright red, orange, or sometimes yellow berries. Plenty of cream- or yellow-variegated types to choose from; the degree of prickliness of the leaves can vary greatly. Height also varies depending on growing conditions.
 Z7–9

EUCALYPTUS GUNNII

Koelreuteria paniculata
(Golden rain tree)
Fine specimen tree, reaching 33ft/10m or more, with divided leaves that are pinkish red as they emerge, become green, and turn butter yellow in autumn. Large spikes of small yellow flowers in summer are followed by rosy, bladderlike fruits. Tolerates drought and wind, but not if salt-laden. Pruning is usually unnecessary and best avoided.
◪ Z6–9

Ligustrum lucidum
(Chinese privet)
An evergreen small tree or large shrub, occasionally reaching 33ft/10m, with glossy leaves and spikes of white flowers in late summer, followed by black fruits. Makes a good specimen plant.
◪ Z8–10

Parkinsonia aculeata
(Jerusalem thorn)
A small, tender, deciduous tree or large shrub from southern US and Mexico. Spiny shoots bear delicate, divided leaves that fold up at night (they will drop during very hot, dry

KOELREUTERIA PANICULATA

spells), and bright yellow flowers in spring. Can reach 33ft/10m tall.
◪ Min. 41°F/5°C

Pinus (Pine)
Many pines do well in dry, windy, and seaside sites. Many make large trees (for instance, *P. parviflora* (Z6–9) grows 33–65ft/10–20m), but look for dwarfer forms more suitable for small gardens. *P. mugo* (dwarf mountain pine, Z3–7) reaches only 11½ft/3.5m, and the shore pine, *P. contorta* (Z6–8), stays shrubby on poor, sandy soil. *P. radiata* (Z7–9) and *P. sylvestris* (Z3–7) make good shelterbelt trees. *P. thunbergii* (Z5–8) makes a rounded tree up to 82ft/25m tall that will tolerate salt spray.
◪
P. thunbergii, see p.33

Quercus (Oak)
Huge range of mostly very large trees requiring a variety of conditions. *Q. ilex* (holly oak, Z7–9) is an evergreen with tough leaves, glossy above and gray-hairy underneath, that are well equipped to withstand drying winds. It can reach 82ft/25m in height with a

PINUS PARVIFLORA

65ft/20m spread. *Q. rubra* (red oak, Z5–9) reaches similar proportions. Fast-growing and deciduous, its leaves usually turn reddish brown in autumn. A good specimen tree needing acidic soil.
◪

Rhus typhina (Staghorn sumac)
An upright, deciduous, small tree or large shrub, up to 16ft/5m tall, that gets its name from its velvety shoots. Divided leaves turn flame-colored in autumn. Yellow-green flowers in summer are followed by conelike clusters of crimson fruits on female plants. Spreads by suckers; can be invasive.
◪ Z3–8

Robinia pseudoacacia
Fast-growing suckering tree, up to 82ft/25m, with deeply divided leaves. Strings of fragrant, white pea flowers are followed by brown seedpods. 'Frisia' has golden foliage turning orange in autumn, but no flowers. 'Idaho' grows to 40ft/12m tall and has dark pink flowers.
◪ Z4–9

RHUS TYPHINA

SHRUBS AND CLIMBERS

SHRUBS PROVIDE a garden's backbone, extending the season of interest. Some are suitable for hedges and screens, sheltering vulnerable plants from drying wind. Like trees, many drought-tolerant shrubs come from the Mediterranean and similar climates and often suffer in cold, damp winters. It is easier to establish young plants in a dry garden; they will make better plants in the long term.

Artemisia

Shrubby types, excellent for hot, dry sites, include *A. abrotanum* (lad's love, Z5–8), an erect plant (to 3ft/1m) with pungent, semi-evergreen, green-gray, leaves, and even more feathery, silvery, 24in/60cm-high A. 'Powis Castle' (Z7–9). Both need cutting back in spring to stop them from getting ungainly.
❂

Atriplex halimus (Tree purslane)

Good seaside shrub that can withstand drying, salt-laden winds. Semi-evergreen, with leathery, silver-gray leaves. Tiny greenish white flowers appear in late summer and autumn. Grows to 6½ft/2m high with an 8ft/2.5m spread.
❂ Z7–9
A. halimus, see p.37

Ballota pseudodictamnus

Shrubby, semi-evergreen plant forming a low, 18in/45cm mound. Gray-green leaves on woolly stems resist drought by curling inward. Whorls of pinkish white flowers appear late spring and early summer.
❂ Z7–9

Bougainvillea glabra

A brilliantly colored evergreen climber for a dry site in a warm climate, where it can reach 26ft/8m, its white or magenta flowers covering walls, arbors, and pergolas. In cold climates it needs a conservatory.
❂ Z9–11

Caragana arborescens (Peashrub)

An upright, thorny deciduous shrub, up to 20ft/6m tall, with divided, light green leaves. Pale yellow pea flowers appear in late spring. 'Nana' has a dwarf, congested habit with twisted shoots, growing to only 5ft/1.5m high.
❂ Z2–8

Cistus (Sun rose)

Evergreen shrubs with a succession of short-lived flowers all summer. Leaves, often aromatic, are frequently gray-green. *C. ladanifer* (Z8–10), one of the most drought resistant, has sticky leaves and crimson-blotched white flowers. It grows to 6½ft/2m tall. *C. × purpureus* (Z9–10), with dark pink flowers with a maroon blotch, makes a bush 3ft/1m tall and wide. Trim after flowering to encourage its rounded shape. *C. salviifolius* 'Prostratus' is low and spreading, no higher than 10in/25cm, with yellow-centered white flowers. All can be rather short-lived, especially on alkaline soil.
❂

Convolvulus cneorum

A compact, bushy shrub, about 24in/60cm high, with silky, silvery leaves. White, funnel-shaped flowers emerge from clusters of pink buds from late spring to early summer. Enjoys baking sun and well-drained soils and will not survive moisture combined

ARTEMISIA 'POWIS CASTLE'

CARAGANA ARBORESCENS 'NANA'

COTONEASTER HORIZONTALIS

with cold. Can be grown in a container, allowing it to be given shelter during winter. ⊡ **Z8–10**
C. cneorum, see p.41

Cotoneaster

Genus of evergreen and semi-evergreen shrubs, including tall types for walls or screens and groundcover plants. Most have inconspicuous flowers followed by masses of berries. Deciduous *C. horizontalis* (Z5–7) is about 3ft/1m high with a wider spread and branches that form a herring-bone pattern. In autumn, it is covered with red berries that attract birds. Evergreen *C. conspicuus* (Z6–8) forms a dense mound, up to 5ft/1.5m tall; its red berries last well into winter. *C. lacteus* (Z7–9) is good for a tall evergreen hedge (trim lightly in late winter). ⊡

Cytisus (Broom)

Deciduous shrubs, varying in size, with prolific clusters of pea flowers in mid- and late spring (see also *Genista*). Flowers are usually cream to bright yellow, occasionally pink or red. *C. × praecox,*

about 4ft/1.2m tall, has arching stems; *C. × kewensis* is about 12in/30cm high and spreading – excellent trailing over banks and retaining walls. All usually succeed on poor soils and must not be pruned hard when mature. ⊡ **Z6–8**

Echinocactus grusonii

(Golden barrel cactus)
Basically round cactus, very slowly achieving a height (about 32in/80cm) larger than its girth of about 24in/60cm. Angular ribs are edged with yellow spines, and it produces bright yellow flowers. To add drama in colder areas, grow it in a container that can be overwintered under glass. ⊡ Min. 50°F/10°C when immature
E. grusonii, see p.37

Elaeagnus

Deciduous *E. angustifolia* (Z3–8) makes a shrub or small tree, about 20ft/6m tall, with narrow silver leaves and tiny clove-scented flowers in summer. 'Quicksilver' has especially silvery leaves. Evergreen *E. macrophylla*

CYTISUS × PRAECOX

ERIOGONUM ARBORESCENS

(Z7–9) tolerates shade and wind. It too bears fragrant flowers, growing up to 10ft/3m. *E. × ebbingei* (Z7–10), also evergreen and slightly taller, makes a good screen. ⊡

Eriogonum

Genus of shrubs with a wide hardiness range. *E. arborescens* (min. 41°F/5°C) is a rounded plant up to 5ft/1.5m. Tufts of leaves are borne at shoot tips, along with white-pink flowers from summer to autumn. In colder climates *E. umbellatum* var. *torreyanum* (Z4–8) makes a spreading shrub, up to 3ft/1m across and 12in/30cm high, with bright yellow flowers. It looks striking in gravel. ⊡

Escallonia

Evergreen shrubs with glossy, dark green leaves. White, pink, or red flowers are borne in summer. A good seaside shrub, resistant to wind and strong sunshine. Trim after flowering to keep in shape. Excellent for hedges and shelterbelts. Height varies but is often around 5–6½ft/1.5–2m. ⊡ **Z8–9**

EUONYMUS FORTUNEI
'SILVER QUEEN'

Euonymus fortunei

Evergreen foliage shrub, about 24in/60cm high, with leaves often splashed with gold or white. 'Silver Queen' is taller – about 8ft/2.5m – and has white-margined, dark green leaves. 'Emerald Gaiety' has similar coloring but grows to about 3ft/1m. 'Emerald 'n' Gold' has yellow-edged leaves.
□ Z5–9

Euphorbia characias

Shrubby member of this huge genus (*see p.60*). Yard-/meter-high stems of blue-green

leaves carry brilliantly contrasting heads of green-yellow flowers from late spring. Cut faded flower stems back to the base. Sticky, milky sap can irritate skin.
□ Z7–10
E. characias, see p.46

Fremontodendron californicum

A vigorous evergreen shrub with striking yellow flowers from late spring to autumn. *F.* 'California Glory' is a hardier, even more spectacular hybrid with deeper yellow flowers and a more spreading habit. Plant against a sunny, sheltered wall in marginal areas. Will reach about 20ft/6m high. Foliage can irritate skin.
□ Z8–10

Genista (Broom)

Genus of mostly deciduous shrubs with yellow pea flowers, very similar to *Cytisus*. *G. hispanica* (Spanish gorse, Z7–9) forms dense, prickly mounds, about 30in/75cm high, with flower spikes at the shoot tips in late spring and early summer. *G. aetnensis* (Mount Etna broom, Z9–10)

× HALIMIOCISTUS WINTONENSIS
'MERRIST WOOD CREAM'

is a large shrub or small tree that can grow to 26ft/8m high, with elegant, weeping branches and fragrant flowers in mid- to late summer.
□
Genista aetnensis, see p.6

Griselinia littoralis

Evergreen shrub with glossy, pale green leaves. Grow in mild seaside gardens as a hedge or as part of a shelter-belt. Height varies according to growing conditions. Trim hedges in summer with pruners. Leaves can have cream variegation.
□ Z8–9

× Halimiocistus wintonensis

Spreading shrub, a cross between *Cistus* and *Halimium*, with green or gray-green leaves and saucer-shaped white flowers with dark crimson bands; 'Merrist Wood Cream' has creamy yellow, red-banded blooms. Low growing, about 24in/60cm, and excellent in raised beds or at the front of borders.
□ Z7–9

EUPHORBIA CHARACIAS SUBSP. WULFENII

Halimium

A smaller version of × *Halimiocistus*, with the same kind of saucer-shaped flowers. It is especially suitable for containers on hot, sunny patios. Reaches 18in/45cm high with a slightly wider spread.
▣ Z9–10

Hebe

This genus includes several plants that make good groundcovers or container shrubs. *H. ochracea* (Z8–10) is small and neat, growing to 18in/45cm. Its stems covered with tiny leaves resemble whipcord. On 'James Stirling' these are ochre-yellow. White flowers appear in spring and early summer. *H. albicans* (Z9–10) makes a 24in/60cm, evergreen mound of gray-green leaves, with white flowers in early summer. The leaves of slightly smaller *H.* 'Red Edge' (Z9–10) lose their red veining as its lilac flowers appear. *H.* 'Youngii' (Z8–9) makes an evergreen, 10in/25cm mound with violet flowers in midsummer. The glaucous

HEBE OCHRACEA
'JAMES STIRLING'

HEDERA COLCHICA 'DENTATA'

foliage of *H. pinguifolia* 'Pagei' (Z8–10) makes an evergreen groundcover, 12in/30cm high, with white flowers from midsummer.
▣
H. 'Red Edge', see p.40

Hedera (Ivy)

Useful in shade, these easy evergreen climbers can also be grown as groundcovers, the variegated types adding brightness to dull areas. *H. colchica* has large, leathery, dark green leaves and can grow to 33ft/10m. 'Dentata' has bright green leaves and stems that are flushed purple. The smaller-leaved English ivy, *H. helix*, has many variations in leaf shape and coloring, including some that are rather tender.
▣ ▣ Z5–10

Helianthemum (Rock rose, sun rose)

Small, low, spreading, usually evergreen shrubs. *H. apenninum* has white flowers with bright yellow centers from spring to mid-summer. There are also numerous hybrids with pink,

yellow, orange, or scarlet flowers. Versatile plants for border fronts, rock gardens, and raised beds. They also make good groundcovers for sunny slopes.
▣ Z6–8

Hippophae rhamnoides

(Sea buckthorn)
A deciduous large shrub or small tree, up to 20ft/6m tall, with spiny shoots carrying narrow, gray-green leaves. Small yellow flowers appear in spring; plant both male and female plants to ensure orange berries. Excellent for hedges or windbreaks in coastal areas and for stabilizing sand dunes.
▣ Z3–8

Hydrangea paniculata

A large deciduous shrub, about 10ft/3m high. Stems are topped by dense, conical heads of creamy white flowers in late summer and early autumn. For the largest flowerheads, cut the previous season's shoots back to a woody framework in spring.
▣ Z4–8

HIPPOPHAE
RHAMNOIDES

HYSSOPUS OFFICINALIS

Hypericum calycinum
(Aaron's beard)
A dwarf, semi-evergreen
shrub, about 24in/60cm high,
with bright yellow flowers
from midsummer to mid-
autumn. It spreads by runners
and is a good groundcover
for dry banks. Invasive, but
useful in that it tolerates shade.
▣ ▣ **Z5–9**

Hyssopus officinalis
(Hyssop)
A dwarf, semi-evergreen,
aromatic shrub bearing
slender spikes of deep blue,
occasionally pink or white,
flowers from late summer to
early autumn. Grows to
about 24in/60cm. Hyssop has
a variety of herbal uses as
well as being decorative.
▣ **Z6–9**

Juniperus (Juniper)
A genus of evergreen conifers
for a wide range of sites.
J. procumbens (Z5–9) is one
of the most successful for
small, dry gardens, particularly
on sandy soil or in windswept
areas. It hugs the ground,
reaching only 30in/75cm high
but spreading to about

6½ft/2m, and has yellow-green
needles. Slightly smaller *J.* ×
pfitzeriana 'Pfitzeriana Aurea'
(Z4–9) looks golden in all but
the depths of winter, when the
leaves turn slightly greener.
▣

Lantana
Tender evergreen shrubs that
can be used as groundcovers
in warm, frost-free climates.
In colder regions grow in a
pot and take under cover in
winter. *L. camara* has rounded
heads of small flowers in a
wide range of eye-catching
colors, often combining two or
more shades. *L. montevidensis*
forms dense mats of foliage, up
to 3ft/1m high, with lilac-pink
to violet flowers in summer.
▣ Min. 50°F/10°C
L. montevidensis, see p.36

Lavandula (Lavender)
Intensely aromatic evergreen
shrubs (up to 3ft/1m tall) with
fragrant, pale to deep purple
flowers in mid- to late summer.
Flowers can also be pink or
white; in some plants, the
narrow leaves are particularly
silvery. *L. angustifolia*,

English lavender, is the
hardiest (Z5–8). *L. stoechas*
(French lavender) is hardy in
Z8–9 and has curious dark
purple flowers topped by
purple bracts; it grows to
24in/60cm. Use lavender for
edging or as a low hedge.
Trim plants in spring to
prevent their getting leggy;
avoid cutting into old wood.
Old plants become ungainly
and should be replaced.
▣
L. angustifolia 'Twickel
Purple', *see p.18*

Lavatera
Shrubs (as well as annuals,
biennials, and perennials) often
found growing in the wild in
dry, rocky places. 'Barnsley'
(Z7–9) is vigorous and semi-
evergreen, reaching 6½ft/2m,
with gray-green leaves and a
graceful habit. White flowers,
with a deep pink eye, appear
in profusion from midsummer
and slowly turn soft pink.
Plants soon become leggy and
are best pruned while young.
They are often cut back by
cold but usually reshoot.
▣

LAVATERA 'BARNSLEY'

Lonicera periclymenum
(Honeysuckle)
Beautifully fragrant white to yellow flowers, often flushed red, appear in mid- to late summer. A deciduous, twining climber that can reach 23ft/7m. The flowers of 'Serotina' (late Dutch) are streaked with reddish purple. 'Graham Thomas' has white flowers, turning yellow. Cut back hard after flowering to produce new shoots near the base.
◻ ◻ Z5–9

Lotus hirsutus
Attractive small, shrubby plant, about 24in/60cm high. Evergreen or semi-evergreen gray-green leaves are softly coated with silver hairs. The pealike, pinkish white flowers in summer and early autumn develop into reddish brown seedpods. May not survive a wet winter.
◻ Z6–9

Nerium oleander
Leggy shrub or small tree, about 6½ft/2m high or more in favorable climates, with narrow green or gray-green

LONICERA PERICLYMENUM
'SEROTINA'

OPUNTIA ROBUSTA

leaves. A profusion of red, pink, or white flowers appear throughout summer. Although it can withstand drought, it is susceptible to wind damage so should not be allowed to become leggy. Needs a protected spot in marginal areas and tolerates some shade. All parts are toxic.
◻ Min. 36°F/2°C

Olearia
Mainly evergreen shrubs or small trees with white daisy flowers. O. macrodonta and O. × haastii (both Z9–10) are suitable for hedging and shelterbelts in windswept and seaside areas. Trim in mid- to late spring. O. macrodonta, up to 20ft/6m tall, has holly-like leaves and flowers in summer. O. × haastii (up to 6½ft/2m) flowers from midsummer; its glossy leaves are felted underneath. O. × scilloniensis (Z8–10), also 6½ft/2m high, flowers in late spring.
◻

Opuntia robusta
One of the many prickly pear cacti – architectural and dramatic when it takes on a

treelike shape at about 6½ft/2m. Oval stem sections (pads) are covered in tufts of spines. Yellow flowers in summer are followed by red fruits. It can tolerate 25°F/-4°C outdoors if grown in very well-drained soil without winter moisture. Alternatively, grow in a container and overwinter under glass. Slow-growing.
◻
O. robusta, see p.37

Ozothamnus rosmarinifolius
A compact, erect shrub, usually 6½–10ft/2–3m high, with needlelike leaves. Fragrant white flowers emerge from red buds in early summer. Avoid planting in heavy soils that are wet in winter.
◻ Z8–10

Parahebe catarractae
An evergreen shrubby plant with small leaves tinged purple when young and flowers throughout summer. About 12in/30cm high and wide, it makes a fine plant for gravel gardens and border fronts.
◻ Z9–10

PARAHEBE
CATARRACTAE

PEROVSKIA 'BLUE SPIRE'

ROMNEYA COULTERI
'WHITE CLOUD'

Perovskia

Upright, deciduous shrubs, with striking, gray-white stems and silver-gray leaves. Long spikes of violet-blue flowers appear in late summer and early autumn. Usually reaches about 4ft/1.2m. Cut back to near the base in spring. Useful in containers, on dry, alkaline soil, and on the coast.
🔲 Z6–9
P. 'Hybrida', see p.19

Phlomis

This genus includes shrubs and herbaceous perennials. P. fruticosa (Jerusalem sage, Z8–9) is a rounded, evergreen shrub, about 3ft/1m high, with yellow flowers in early and midsummer among gray-green leaves. An architectural plant, useful for containers. P. italica (Z9–10) has lilac-pink flowers and silvery, felted leaves. (See also P. russeliana, p.62.)
🔲

Prunus laurocerasus

(Cherry laurel)
Thick, glossy evergreen shrub, 26ft/8m tall and wide but spreading more with age. Spikes of small, fragrant white

flowers are produced in mid- to late spring, followed by cherrylike red fruits that ripen to black. Makes a dense hedge; it withstands hard pruning, preferably with pruners.
🔲 Z6–9

Romneya coulteri

(Tree poppy)
Large, papery, white flowers with bright yellow centers are produced nearly all summer above attractive gray-green foliage. Deciduous, and needs free-draining soil plus the protection of a sheltered wall in marginal areas. May be difficult to establish, but when growing well it can sucker extensively and may become invasive. Will reach 3–8ft/1–2.5m high.
🔲 Z7–8

Rosa (Rose)

Most roses need reasonably moist conditions, but a few of the species cope with dry conditions and salty winds. R. rugosa (Z2–9) is a vigorous rose with wrinkled, leathery leaves. Grows 3–6½ft/1–2m tall and makes a splendid,

intruder-proof hedge. Single, scented, violet-carmine flowers are followed by showy red hips. R. rugosa var. alba has white flowers. R. pimpinellifolia (burnet rose, Z3–9) has very small, fernlike leaves, lots of prickles, and single, creamy white flowers followed by black hips. Suckering, it grows to about 3ft/1m tall.
🔲

Rosmarinus officinalis

(Rosemary)
Evergreen shrub with intensely aromatic, needlelike leaves. Tubular blue flowers cover the stems in spring; there may be a second flush in autumn. Will grow to 5ft/1.5m tall, but can get straggly; prune if necessary after flowering. Can be grown as a hedge and trimmed after flowering. Trailing or prostrate forms grow to only 6in/15cm high – excellent for banks and raised beds but often less hardy.
🔲 Z8–10

Ruta graveolens (Rue)

Evergreen shrub grown for its filigree, pungent, blue-green foliage; yellow flowers appear

ROSA RUGOSA

SANTOLINA
CHAMAECYPARISSUS

TAMARIX RAMOSISSIMA
'PINK CASCADE'

in summer. Grows to 3ft/1m high. Clip off flower buds for the best foliage. Contact with foliage in sun can cause skin to blister badly.
■ Z5–9

Santolina (Lavender cotton) Compact, evergreen, rounded shrubs covered with bright yellow or lemon buttonlike flowers in mid- to late summer. Foliage is better if the flowers are removed before they open. *S. chamaecyparissus* (Z6–9) grows to about 20in/50cm high and has white-woolly shoots and finely divided, aromatic, silvery leaves. Suitable for a low hedge. Trim in late spring. *S. pinnata* (Z9–10) is slightly larger with green or gray-green leaves. Prune in spring to prevent it from sprawling; avoid cutting into old wood.
■
S. pinnata 'Edward Bowles', *see p.18*

Spartium junceum (Spanish broom) An upright shrub, up to 10ft/3m tall. The thin, sparsely leaved stems bear fragrant

yellow pea flowers from summer to early autumn. Flattened brown seedpods follow the flowers. Thrives by the coast and on alkaline soil. Where marginal, grow in the shelter of a sunny wall. Trim lightly in spring, if necessary.
■ Z8–10

Tamarix (Tamarisk) Graceful shrubs or small trees, from 10–16ft/3–5m tall, with arching stems and delicate feathery foliage. Plumes of small pink flowers appear on *T. ramosissima* (Z3–8) in late summer and early autumn; *T. tetrandra* (Z5–9) flowers in spring. Plants grow well on sandy soil and make an excellent hedge or windbreak in exposed coastal regions.
■

Teucrium fruticans Evergreen shrub with an open habit, growing to 3ft/1m tall. Small, silvery, aromatic leaves clothe branching stems, and lipped, pale blue flowers appear in summer. Needs well-drained soil and benefits from the shelter of a sunny

wall. In warm climates, can be grown as a hedge. Clip in spring.
■ Z8–9

Ulex europaeus (Furze, gorse, whin) Dense, bushy shrub, up to 8ft/2.5m, with viciously spiny leaves and stem tips. Bright yellow pea flowers are produced intermittently all year but are at their peak in spring. A plant that likes poor, sandy, acidic to neutral soil, and can be invasive. Use to form an impenetrable low hedge, and trim after flowering every other year.
■ Z6–8

Yucca Dramatic and architectural plants with evergreen sword-like leaves and spikes of white bells in summer. Leaves may be striped yellow or cream. *Y. filamentosa* (Z5–10) reaches 30in/75cm (taller in flower); *Y. gloriosa* (Z7–10) reaches 6½ft/2m. *Y. whipplei* (Z7–9), reaching about 3ft/1m, has slender gray-green leaves.
■
Y. whipplei, see p.36

TEUCRIUM FRUTICANS 'COMPACTUM'

PERENNIALS AND BULBS

DROUGHT-TOLERANT PERENNIALS seldom produce the same sort of luxuriant growth as traditional herbaceous border plants, so they require less staking and cutting back, other than to deadhead. A few need all-year warmth; in cold climates overwinter them in a greenhouse, conservatory, or cold frame. Many rock garden plants (*see p.66*) are also ideal for border edges and containers.

Acanthus
Handsome plants with large, divided leaves. Spires of hooded, tubular flowers in white, green, dusky purple, or pink appear on stems up to 4ft/1.2m tall. Summer-flowering *A. spinosus* (Z5–9) has very deeply cut leaves in clumps up to 5ft/1.5m across.
◘

Achillea (Yarrow)
Spreading or clump-forming genus of perennials with attractive fernlike, gray or green leaves. Long-lasting, large, flat flowerheads, in shades of yellow or palest peach to deep red, are carried on strong stems from early summer to early autumn. Some, such as 'Moonshine' (Z4–8) and *A. filipendulina* 'Gold Plate'

(Z3–8), are evergreen; heights vary from 24in/60cm to 4ft/1.2m. Grow well on poor, dry soil. Flowers can be dried for winter decoration.
◘
A. millefolium 'Sammetriese', *see p.30*

Agapanthus
Sturdy stems crowned with round heads of blue or white flowers rise from clumps of straplike leaves in summer. Headbourne hybrids are the hardiest (Z6–9) but variable in color; flower stems reach 32in/80cm. 'Loch Hope' produces deep blue flowers in late summer on 5ft/1.5m stems. Much smaller 'Blue Moon' (Z8–10) is good in pots.
◘ Z6–10
A. 'Blue Moon', see p.40

Agave
Tender succulents with stiff, fleshy leaves, sometimes variegated and usually tipped with a vicious spine. The grayish green leaves of *A. americana* (min 41°F/5°C) are up to 6½ft/2m long and have pale yellow margins in 'Marginata'. *A. filifera* (min. 50°F/10°C) has rosettes of slender leaves up to 10in/25cm long. Plants survive better outside in marginal regions in well-drained soil. *Agave* can be grown in pots.
◘

Allium
A group of ornamental onions, usually with round heads of small starry flowers in mauves, pinks, yellow, or white. Strappy leaves die back as the flowers appear. Most thrive in sandy, dry soil. *A. caeruleum* (Z4–10) has blue flowers on 24in/60cm stems in early summer. *A. cristophii* (Z5–8) is a similar height but with heads up to 8in/20cm in diameter of metallic pink-purple flowers in early summer.
◘ Z7–10
A. cristophii, see p.31

Aloe
Showy, tender succulents producing rosettes of thick tapering leaves. *A. ferox* grows very slowly to 13ft/4m and looks like a single-stemmed

ACHILLEA FILIPENDULINA 'GOLD PLATE'

ALLIUM CAERULEUM

ASCLEPIAS TUBEROSA

tree crowned by glaucous, spiny leaves. *A. aristata* has dense rosettes of fleshy leaves and 24in-/60cm-high spires of orange-red flowers. Like *Agave* (*opposite*) these can be grown outside in mild, exceptionally well-drained areas, or in pots. ☐ Min. 50°F/10°C
A. ferox, see p.37

Anthemis
Perennials (and some annuals) forming clumps of parsleylike, aromatic foliage. White or yellow daisy flowers have a long season from late spring or early summer. *A. punctata* subsp. *cupaniana* (Z6–9) has fine, feathery, gray foliage. ☐
A. tinctoria 'E.C. Buxton', see p.6

Artemisia
Invaluable range of perennials and shrubs (*see p.50*) for hot sites. Many make a good groundcover, their silver foliage setting off other plants. *A. stelleriana* (Z3–7) resists drying winds and strong sun. Evergreen, it reaches 6in/15cm high, spreading to 18in/45cm. ☐

Asclepias tuberosa
(Butterfly weed)
Clusters of orange-red flowers, sometimes yellow, are carried on strong stems, up to 3ft/1m tall, from midsummer to early autumn. The flowers, attractive to butterflies and bees, are followed by spindle-shaped green fruits.
☐ **Z4–9**

Asphodeline lutea
(Yellow asphodel)
Stiff spikes of yellow, starry flowers up to 5ft/1.5m tall emerge from clumps of blue-gray, grassy leaves. Stems become beaded with green cherrylike fruits, which later turn brown. The leaves tend to die down and disappear after midsummer and reshoot in early autumn.
☐ **Z6–9**
A. lutea, see pp.28, 31

Calamintha nepeta
A tough groundcover plant, also good for gravel gardens. Grows up to 18in/45cm. Leaves smell minty, and the profusion of tiny lilac flowers in summer and autumn

DICTAMNUS ALBUS VAR. PURPUREA

CRAMBE MARITIMA

attract bees. The flowers of 'Blue Cloud' are a good deep blue.
☐ **Z5–9**
C. nepeta, see p.19

Crambe
Clump-forming perennials that bear clouds of tiny white flowers. The mounds of large, puckered leaves produced by *C. cordifolia* die down in midsummer as the 8ft/2.5m flower stems emerge. Seakale, *C. maritima*, has glaucous leaves; shoots can be blanched in late winter, steamed, and eaten as a vegetable.
☐ **Z6–9**
C. maritima, see pp.16, 18

Dictamnus albus
(Gas plant)
Pretty spires of white or pale pink flowers are produced in early summer above clumps of divided leaves. Height can vary from 16–36in/40–90cm. In hot, still weather, a flammable vapor is produced. This can be ignited near the leaves without damaging the plant. Contact with skin may cause photodermatitis.
☐ **Z3–8**

ERYNGIUM ALPINUM

Echinacea purpurea
(Purple coneflower)
An easy-to-grow plant that
adds to the color of the late
summer garden. Distinctive
mauve-pink or white daisies
have high central domes of
orange-brown.
▣ Z3–9
E. purpurea 'Robert Bloom',
see p.31

Echinops (Globe thistle)
Spiny-leaved, clump-forming
plants with round, metallic
blue flowerheads in summer.
E. bannaticus (Z5–9) may
reach 3ft/1m; *E. ritro* (Z3–9)
is shorter (up to 24in/60cm)
with flowers aging to a darker
blue. 'Veitch's Blue' has a
slightly longer flowering
season. Flowers dry well for
indoor arrangements or look
handsome left on the plant.
▣
E. ritro, see p.30

Epimedium (Barrenwort)
Invaluable groundcover plants
that tolerate dry shade. Can
be evergreen or deciduous, up
to 10in/25cm tall, with glossy
leaves sometimes bronze-
tinted in spring and autumn.

Dainty flowers, often spurred,
appear from early spring to
early summer in yellow, beige,
white, pink, red, or purple.
E. × versicolor (Z5–9) is one
of the most tolerant of dry soil
and sun. Shear early in spring
to promote fresh growth.
▣

Eryngium (Sea holly)
Large genus of perennials
(also some annuals and
biennials), usually with deep
taproots and basal rosettes of
spiny, veined leaves. In
summer, round or egg-shaped,
white or blue flowerheads are
held above attractive ruffs of
spiky bracts. *E. giganteum* is
short-lived and often grown as
a biennial. It reaches about
3ft/1m and self-seeds liberally.
E. alpinum is shorter with
very handsome flower ruffs.
E. × oliverianum, a cross
between these two, has well-
marked veining. Leave faded
flowerheads for winter display.
▣ Z5–8
E. giganteum, see p.18
E. maritimum, see p.33

Erysimum (Wallflowers)
Evergreens with narrow gray-
green leaves and spikes of
mauve, orange, red, yellow,
or cream flowers from late
winter to early summer. Woody
stems can get very leggy, and
plants need annual renewing.
Plants reach 10–30in/25–75cm.
▣ Z3–7

Euphorbia (Spurge)
Diverse genus, often with
striking blue-green foliage and
contrasting yellow-green
flowerheads. Drought-tolerant
perennials include *E. myrsinites*
(Z5–8) with succulent, pointed
leaves on almost prostrate

stems, arranged like spiders'
legs. Bright greenish yellow
flowers appear at the stem
tips in spring. *E. nicaeensis*
(Z5–8) has similar foliage but
is bushy and upright, with
flowers from spring to midsummer. *E. griffithii* (Z4–9)
about 30cm/75cm high, has
orange-red flowerheads in
early summer and leaves that
take on red and yellow tints
in autumn. A spreading plant,
it can be invasive. Milky sap
can cause skin irritation. (*See
also E. characias, p.52.*)
▣
E. myrsinites, see p.19
E. griffithii, see pp.28, 31

Gaillardia
Bushy perennials, often short-
lived, found growing on the
prairies of North America.
Colorful flowers are set off
by the gray-green leaves. Easy
to grow. *G. × grandiflora*
reaches about 3ft/1m and
produces yellow daisy flowers,
banded with red, from early
summer to early autumn.
'Dazzler' has orange-red
flowers with yellow tips
and a maroon center.
▣ Z3–8

GAILLARDIA × GRANDIFLORA

GAZANIA CHANSONETTE SERIES

Gazania
Bright daisy flowers are produced all summer but open only when the sun is out. Spreading plants are about 8in/20cm high. Though perennial, best treated as an annual in warm areas. Evergreen leaves are covered with silky white hairs underneath. The flowers come in shades of bronze-orange, salmon, orange, yellow, and rose, often banded with green. Excellent plants for containers.
⚙ Z8–10
Harlequin Hybrids, *see p.41*

Helichrysum
Large group of perennials, some grown purely for their attractive woolly or hairy foliage, others also for their clusters of small, papery flowers. *H.* 'Schwefellicht' (Z9–10) forms silvery clumps of foliage with sulfur yellow flowers in late summer, up to 16in/40cm tall. *H. petiolare* (Z7–10) has long, trailing stems of evergreen gray-green leaves, especially useful in containers but best treated as an annual in most areas.
⚙

Iris
Several types of iris enjoy dry conditions, including the bearded irises. They come in a range of sizes – dwarf, intermediate, and tall. Irises offer a wide choice of color in their flowers, some with ruffled petals. The handsome spears of foliage grow out of surface-rooting rhizomes that like to bake in the sun and need regular division in late summer.
⚙ Z3–9

Kniphofia (Red-hot poker)
Striking flower spikes in lemon, orange, or red shoot up in summer from clumps of straplike leaves. Versatile plants, able to grow well in a wide range of conditions, but needing plenty of organic matter added to poor, dry soil to help them survive long periods of drought.
⚙ Z5–9

Lamium
Spreading plants, good as low groundcovers in dry shade (where they are less invasive than in damp conditions). *L. maculatum* grows to 8in/20cm with a 3ft/1m spread and has pink flowers in summer. 'White Nancy' is a similar size with white flowers and silvery leaves edged green.
⚙ Z4–8
L. maculatum, see p.34

Lampranthus
Low-growing succulents covered in summer with bright daisy flowers. Native to the semi-desert areas of South Africa, they are ideal in arid-landscape gardens but must be overwintered under glass in cold climates.

L. haworthii has large pink-purple flowers all summer, and pale green foliage frosted with gray. Grows to 20in/50cm high with a wider spread. *L. spectabilis* is slightly lower growing and is available in a range of apricots and reds.
⚙ Min. 45°F/7°C
L. haworthii, see p.36

Limonium platyphyllum
(Sea lavender)
Rosettes of spoon-shaped leaves are topped, in late summer, by masses of tiny lavender-blue flowers, useful in dried flower arrangements. These are borne on 24in/60cm branching, wiry stems. A good plant for dry coastal areas and sandy soil.
⚙ Z4–9

Lychnis
These originate from a variety of habitats; those with the most silvery foliage generally tolerate the driest conditions. *L. flos-jovis* (Z4–8) forms mats of grayish leaves with white, pink, or scarlet flowers, 8–24in/20–60cm high, from early to late summer.
⚙

LIMONIUM LATIFOLIUM

NEPETA SIBIRICA

Nepeta (Catmint)
An extremely useful group of perennials, usually blue-flowered and with aromatic leaves. *N. sibirica* (Z3–8) is well able to withstand drought. It grows to 3ft/1m and bears lavender-blue flowers above dark green leaves from mid- to late summer. *N. × faassenii* (Z4–8) has seemingly never-ending sprays of lavender-blue flowers, at their best in mid-summer, above 18in-/45cm-high clumps of silvery gray leaves. Shear back after flowering to keep plants neat and encourage more flowers. ▣
N. × faassenii, see p.31

Oenothera (Evening primrose)
Yellow, occasionally white or pink, cup-shaped flowers open at dawn or dusk, fade quickly but usually appear over a long period. Most perennial species grow well in sunny, well-drained sites. *O. macrocarpa* (Z5–8) has trailing, red-tinted stems, 6in/15cm high but spreading to 20in/50cm, with yellow flowers from late spring to autumn. ▣

Origanum, see p.67

Ornithogalum umbellatum
(Star of Bethelehem)
Bulbous plant with open clusters of star-shaped white flowers, striped green on the outside, in early summer. Silver-striped leaves fade as the flowers open. Can reach 12in/30cm high. Invasive. ▣ Z5–10

Pachysandra terminalis
Low, spreading evergreen, up to 8in/20cm high, with glossy, toothed leaves clustered at the ends of the stems and tiny white flowers in early summer. An excellent plant for dry soil in shade, especially under trees. ▣ Z6–9

Phlomis russeliana
Produces weed-smothering clumps of large, hairy leaves. Sturdy stems, up to 3ft/1m tall, bear cream and butter yellow hooded flowers that open from mid- to late summer. If left on the plants, the brown seedheads will decorate the garden in winter. ▣ Z4–9

OENOTHERA MACROCARPA

PHLOMIS RUSSELIANA

Phormium
(New Zealand flax)
Dramatic evergreen plants with sword-shaped leaves. Several color variations are available, including all-bronze or copper- or yellow-striped leaves. *P. tenax* forms clumps of 10ft-/3m-long leaves with taller spikes of dull red flowers in summer. Where hardy, plants are more likely to survive winter cold if the roots are mulched and in light, well-drained soil. You can also wrap leaves in a sheath of burlap or bubble-wrap to protect them further. ▣ Z9–10

Salvia
These useful plants require a variety of conditions; the following suit sunny, dry sites. From mid- to late summer, *S. × superba* (Z5–9) produces 3ft/1m-tall spikes of violet flowers with red bracts that persist after the petals fall. *S. argentea* (Z5–8) could be grown purely for its furry, tactile leaves, which form large, silver rosettes. Good on gravel but needs protection

from winter moisture. (*See also S. sclarea, p.69.*)

❖

Saponaria

Perennials and annuals for dry soils, varying in height from 2–30in/5–75cm. *S. officinalis* (soapwort) grows to 24in/60cm high, with pink, red, or white flowers in summer and autumn. Those such as pink-flowered *S. × olivana*, which form spreading mats of foliage, are good for troughs, dry walls, and rock gardens.
❖ Z5–8

Sedum

Most sedums attract bees and butterflies. At flowering time, plants can have a tendency to sprawl. Clumps of fleshy stems with slightly scalloped, gray-green leaves are topped in late summer with flattish heads of star-shaped flowers. 'Ruby Glow' (Z5–9) has dusky red flowers and grows to 10in/25cm high. 'Bertram Anderson' (Z5–9) is a similar height and has purple foliage and flowers. *S. spectabile* (ice plant, Z4–9) has pink flowers on 45cm stems. There are also

TULIPA TARDA

VERBASCUM OLYMPICUM

several small sedums grown as rock garden plants (*see p.67*).
❖
S. 'Bertram Anderson', *see p.18;*
S. 'Ruby Glow', *see p.40*

Stachys

The leaves of *S. byzantina* (lambs' ears, Z4–8) form carpets of soft, woolly gray; spikes of pink flowers appear in midsummer. 'Silver Carpet' is a fine nonflowering silver foliage plant. *S. candida* (Z5–8) is a small, spreading, shrubby plant, up to 6in/15cm high, with rounded, felted, gray-green leaves. White flowers streaked with purple are produced in summer. Excellent for gravel gardens and is best not exposed to winter moisture.
❖

Tulipa

For many tulips hot, dry summers are essential. These include low-growing *T. tarda*, *T. greigii*, and *T. kaufmanniana*. The Darwin hybrids and other taller bedding tulips also cope well with dry conditions.
❖ Z4–7

Verbascum

Large genus of perennials (plus a few annuals and biennials), with spikes of yellow, white, or pink flowers that shoot up from basal rosettes of leaves. These are often gray-green. *V. olympicum* has woolly, whitish leaves with imposing 6½ft/2m-high candelabras of yellow flowers in late summer. It may die after flowering. *V. chaixii* 'Pink Domino' has dark, purplish green leaves and 28in/70cm spikes of rose-pink flowers from early to late summer.
❖ Z5–9

Verbena bonariensis

An extremely useful plant for late summer and autumn, when clusters of small rosy purple flowers appear on wiry, branching stems, to 6½ft/2m tall. Can be used to create flowering screens through which you can see other parts of the garden. It is not reliably hardy but often self-seeds itself among other plants in an attractive, serendipitous way.
❖ Z7–11
V. bonariensis, see p.18

VERBENA BONARIENSIS

ORNAMENTAL GRASSES

NOT ALL GRASSES ARE DROUGHT TOLERANT – some need moist soil – but those that want dry conditions deserve a place in the garden for the way they bend in the wind, catch the sunlight, and look magnificent beaded with dew or rimed with frost. They come in a whole range of sizes; unless stated otherwise, those below are perennial. Many are evergreen, giving all-year decoration.

Briza (Quaking grass)
Forms dense clumps of foliage with heart-shaped flowers that quake in the breeze. *B. media* (Z4–10) is perennial, with blue-green leaves and nodding flowers in summer, on 24in/60cm stems; they turn straw-colored as they mature. ▣

Cortaderia selloana
(Pampas grass)
A spectacular grass with tall plumes of silky flowers, often flushed pink or purple, in late summer. Flower stems can reach 10ft/3m high. 'Pumila' makes a smaller plant. The sharp-edged leaves form dense evergreen clumps. Plants look good in minimalist designs with decking and cobblestones.
▣ Z7–10

CORTADERIA SELLOANA
'AUREOLINEATA'

Elymus hispidus
(Blue wheatgrass)
An evergreen perennial with narrow, intensely blue leaves that grow to about 24in/60cm. Erect at first, these spread out later. The wheatlike flower spikes are the same brilliant blue at first but quickly fade to a yellow-beige. The blue-gray leaves of *E. magellanicus* are covered in a whitish bloom.
▣ Z7–9

Eragrostis curvula
(Love grass)
A perennial that makes large, graceful clumps with arching, rough-textured, dark green leaves up to 4ft/1.2m tall. In late summer it forms a haze of nodding spikelets, which persist to give a metallic gray effect above wintry buff stems.
▣ Z9–10

Festuca glauca (Blue fescue)
A perennial grass growing in dense clumps. The very fine blades range from green to intense steely blue. *F. glauca* forms neat mounds of powder blue leaves up to 12in/30cm high. Spikelets of violet-flushed, blue-green flowers appear in early and midsummer. 'Elijah Blue' has eye-catching steely blue leaves, to 8in/20cm, and blue-gray flowers. 'Blaufuchs' has bright blue leaves.
▣ Z4–8
F. ovina, see p.33

Helictotrichon sempervirens
(Blue oat grass)
A densely tufted grass that forms a mound of narrow, gray-blue leaves. Evergreen, though it can look rather tattered in winter. Spikelets of straw-colored flowers, marked with purple, are borne on stiff, 4½ft/1.4m stems in early and midsummer.
▣ Z4–9

Holcus mollis
'Albovariegatus'
A creeping plant with tufts of flat, blue-green and cream leaves, up to 8in/20cm tall. It gives the overall effect of a carpet of white, especially in spring. Spikes of pale green flowers are borne in summer.
▣ ▣ Z5–9

FESTUCA GLAUCA

HELICTOTRICHON
SEMPERVIRENS

Koeleria glauca
(Glaucous hair grass)
Evergreen tufts of narrow,
silver-blue leaves with inrolled
margins reach about 8in/20cm
high. Shiny spikelets of cream
and green flowers in early
and midsummer gradually
turn buff-colored with age.
▣ Z6–9

Leymus arenarius
(Lyme grass)
Although fast-spreading in
dry gardens, sometimes
invasively so, it is desirable
where it can be contained or
given room for its broad blue-
green leaves. They grow to
24in/60cm high. Tall, stiff,
wheatlike flower spikes are
borne throughout summer.
▣ Z4–9

Melica altissima
A dainty, erect, noninvasive
perennial making soft-leaved
clumps. 'Atropurpurea'
produces 3ft-/1m-tall spikes
of deep purple flowers in
midsummer, which fall
charmingly to one side and
fade to rosy pink when dried.
▣ Z5–8

Pennisetum (Fountain grass)
A fountain effect is created by
the way the fluffy, foxtail
flowerheads rise up on
slender stems from nicely
rounded mounds of leaves.
P. alopecuroides (Z6–9) is
perennial and evergreen,
making graceful clumps
about 30in/75cm high of
arching, bright green leaves.
The brownish purple
bottlebrush flowers rise about
3ft/1m above the leaves in
autumn and early winter,
supplying the garden with
marvelous color. They pale
with age but last through the
winter. 'Woodside' is very
free-flowering. The dwarf
'Hameln', only 12in/30cm
high, has dark green leaves
that turn golden yellow in
autumn. It flowers freely, but
its stiffish stems lessen the
"fountain" effect. *P. villosum*
(Z9–10) has very soft, fluffy
flowers that emerge silky
green then turn light pink in
color. The narrow green
leaves are about 6in/15cm
long. It is often grown as an
annual in cold areas.
▣

PENNISETUM
VILLOSUM

STIPA GIGANTEA

Schizachyrium scoparium
(Little bluestem)
Clumps of erect mid- to gray-
green leaves turn a purplish
orange-red in autumn. Wispy
3ft-/1m-tall flower spikelets
appear from midsummer to
late autumn.
▣ Z5–9
S. scoparium, see p.19

Stipa
Decorative grasses with
beautiful, often feathery
flowerheads. *S. tenuissima*
(Z7–10) makes dense tufts of
bright green, deciduous leaves.
The wispy flower spikes, up to
24in/60cm tall, are produced
all summer. These gradually
turn a buff color and billow
in the gentlest puff of wind.
The dark green, leathery leaves
of *S. arundinacea* (Z8–10) turn
orange-brown in autumn.
Arching stems, up to 3ft/1m
high, of purplish green flowers
appear from midsummer.
Evergreen or semi-evergreen
S. gigantea (Z8–10) has
6½ft/2m stems with large, open
heads of oatlike flowers that
tremble and glisten in the sun.
▣
S. arundinacea, see p.30

Rock Garden Plants

Most rock garden plants are ideally suited to the dry garden. In their native habitats they survive long periods of drought, intense light, and scant soil, though they do often naturally tuck themselves behind stones or boulders that trap all available moisture and cast a little shade. Many make good candidates for containers and for planting among paving stones or edging paths.

Acaena
A. novae-zelandiae (Z6–8) is a mat-forming evergreen, no higher than 6in/15cm, ideal for covering banks in full sun. Filigree leaves can be green to gray-green. Red burrs follow mid- to late-summer flowers. *A. saccaticupula* 'Blue Haze' (Z7–9) is vigorous with dark red burrs and gray-blue leaves.

Alyssum
Good plants for border fronts and rock and scree gardens. Both *A. montanum* (Z4–9) and *A. wulfenianum* (Z6–9) are spreading evergreens, reaching about 6in/15cm high, with gray-green leaves. Dense heads of tiny yellow or lemon flowers respectively cover the plants in early summer.

ALYSSUM WULFENIANUM

ANTENNARIA DIOICA 'ROSEA'

Antennaria dioica
Forms mats, up to 18in/45cm wide, of semi-evergreen, silvery leaves topped by fluffy, white or pink "everlasting" flowers in late spring and early summer. Makes a good groundcover and can also be grown in wall crevices and paving. The flowerheads may be dried for decoration.
Z5–9

Arabis
Easily grown evergreens with clusters of small white or purple flowers in late spring. *A. caucasica* (Z4–8) forms low mats, up to 20in/50cm wide, of gray-green leaves with white flowers. Good for groundcover and will spread rapidly over dry walls. 'Variegata' has pale yellow leaf margins.

Armeria (Sea pink, thrift)
Eye-catching small, round heads of white or pink-purple flowers are borne in profusion in late spring and early summer above mounds of grasslike leaves. *A. maritima* (Z3–9), found growing wild along sea cliffs, grows to 8in/20cm tall. *A.* 'Bee's Ruby' (Z6–7) has large, bright pink flowers on slightly taller stems. Excellent for gravel gardens.

Aubrieta x cultorum
Low, carpeting plants, spreading to 24in/60cm or more, that tumble over walls and rocks and grow well with very little moisture. Profuse, single or double, white, pink, mauve, or purple flowers are borne in spring. Tiny evergreen leaves can be attractively variegated. Cut back after flowering.
Z5–7

Cerastium tomentosum
(Snow-in-summer)
Very vigorous, low, mat-forming plant with small, woolly, almost white leaves and a profusion of small white flowers in late spring and summer. Tough and will succeed in poor conditions. Cut back as necessary after flowering so that it does not scramble out of control.
Z3–7

Gypsophila repens
A spreading, semi-evergreen perennial, covered with dainty, white or pink flowers for long periods in summer. Grows to 8in/20cm tall with a spread of up to 20in/50cm. 'Dorothy Teacher' is more compact with blue-green leaves and pale pink flowers that darken with age.
◨ Z4–7

Origanum
Genus of decorative, aromatic plants that includes marjoram, the culinary herb. Many have unusual, attractive flowers. *O. amanum* (Z5–8) is a spreading evergreen, up to 8in/20cm high, with pink flowers among green-pink bracts from late summer. *O. laevigatum* (Z7–10) has upright, wiry stems, to 24in/60cm, with sprays of tiny purple flowers from late spring to autumn. Evergreen *O.* 'Kent Beauty' (Z5–8) has trailing stems tipped with pink flowers. There are also gold-leaved or variegated forms. All suit borders, rock gardens, and containers.
◨
O. laevigatum, see p.31

PHLOX SUBULATA 'G.F. WILSON'

Phlox subulata
An evergreen, mat-forming phlox, spreading up to 20in/50cm. Small purple, red, lilac, pink, or white flowers appear in late spring and early summer. Unlike other trailing phloxes, it grows well in dry sites and likes sun.
◨ Z3–8

Rhodanthemum hosmariense
White daisies appear nonstop from spring to autumn on a spreading plant, up to 12in/30cm tall, with silvery foliage.
◨ Z9–10

ORIGANUM 'KENT BEAUTY'

RHODANTHEMUM HOSMARIENSE

Saponaria, see p.63

Sedum
Apart from the *Sedum* grown as herbaceous perennials (*see p.63*), there are several low-growing types suitable for rock gardens and troughs. *S. spathulifolium* 'Purpureum' (Z5–9) forms 4in-/10cm-high mats of red-purple leaves with yellow flowers in summer.
◨
S. spathulifolium 'Purpureum', *see p.33*

Sempervivum
(Hen and chicks)
Fleshy rosettes of green to purple leaves spread to form mats. They provide ground-cover over really shallow soil and grow even on walls and tiled roofs. Thick-stalked, reddish pink flowers appear in summer. The foliage of *S. arachnoideum* (Z5–8) has a cobwebbing of white hairs. All withstand extreme drought.
◨
S. ciliosum, see p.33
S. montanum, S. giuseppii, see pp.40–41

Thymus (Thyme)
These form spreading mats of foliage or small, bushy plants, and the tiny aromatic leaves may be green, gold, or variegated yellow or silver. Flowers, in summer, are white, pink, or purple and adored by bees. *T. vulgaris* 'Silver Posie' makes a short, woody, bushy plant (about 8in/20cm high) with pretty white-margined leaves. *T. serpyllum* is excellent creeping out from cracks between paving slabs or over banks and ow walls.
◨ Z4–9

ANNUALS AND BIENNIALS

THE MAJORITY OF ANNUALS flower all the better in fairly impoverished ground: too rich a soil encourages a lot of foliage. Some annuals can be sown in autumn to give them an early start the following year; many self-seed of their own accord – be strict about pulling out unwanted seedlings. Biennials produce flowers in their second season; they, too, often scatter their own seed.

Argemone (Prickly poppy)
The sprawling stems of
A. grandiflora (Z8–11) carry prickly, glaucous leaves and clusters of slightly scented white poppies in summer. Often annual (sometimes perennial), it can grow to almost 3ft/1m tall. *A. mexicana* reaches the same sort of height. A clump-forming annual, it has blue-green leaves and yellow poppy flowers. Both thrive on poor, sandy or stony soil.

Brachyscome iberidifolia
(Swan river daisy)
A bushy annual, up to 18in/45cm tall, with slender stems and soft, deeply cut leaves. Plants are covered by masses of fragrant blue-purple daisies, sometimes pink or white, all summer long.

Calendula officinalis
(Pot marigold)
A bright annual with orange or yellow daisy flowers in profusion from summer to autumn, especially in poor, well-drained soil. Self-seeds.

Cosmos bipinnatus
Erect branching stems, up to 5ft/1.5m tall, bear delicate, cup-shaped flowers in shades of crimson, pink, and white up until the first frosts. With

ARGEMONE MEXICANA

its soft, ferny leaves, it is a delightful plant for filling border gaps. The flowers of 'Sea Shells' have fluted petals. The shorter-growing Sonata Series is especially suitable for an exposed garden.

COSMOS 'SONATA WHITE'

Dimorphotheca pluvialis
An annual from southern Africa. White daisies, with blue-brown centers and blue undersides, appear above aromatic leaves. Flowers open only in sun. Plants reach about 16in/40cm and are good at the front of borders or in a container in a hot, sunny site.

Eschscholzia californica
(California poppy)
Bright, cup-shaped flowers, mainly yellow or orange but also red, pink, or cream, appear throughout summer above attractive, filigree, blue-green leaves. Plants grow 12in/30cm or taller. Long, curved seedpods follow the flowers. Self-seeds abundantly around the garden.

ESCHSCHOLZIA CALIFORNICA

LINARIA 'NORTHERN LIGHTS'

Lavatera trimestris
(Mallow)
Showy annual with lots of shallow pink or white trumpets all summer and softly hairy leaves. Grows to over a 3ft/1m. 'Pink Beauty', with purple-veined, pale pink flowers, reaches only half that height, and glistening white 'Mont Blanc' is shorter still. (*See also L.* 'Barnsley', *p.54.*)
⬚

Linaria maroccana
(Toadflax)
Erect plant, about 18in/45cm tall, with small, snapdragon-like flowers in summer, mainly purple but also pink or white. Taller and long-flowering 'Northern Lights' includes shades of yellow, pink, salmon, carmine, lavender, and white.
⬚

Linum grandiflorum
(Flowering flax)
Loose spikes of rose-pink flowers top slender plants with narrow gray-green leaves. Grows 16–30in/40–75cm. Useful for softening stronger tones in a border.
⬚

Onopordum acanthium
Extremely architectural, this giant biennial thistle forms a rosette of spiny, gray-green leaves in its first year and 10ft/3m-high branching stems with purple or white flowers in its second summer.
⬚ Z6–9

Papaver (Poppy)
Few annuals are easier, but be ruthless with self-seedlings. *P. rhoeas* Shirley Series, up to 3ft/90cm, comes in clear pinks, oranges, and reds. At half that height, *P. commutatum* is red, blotched black. The opium poppy, *P. somniferum*, about 3ft/90cm tall, has bluish foliage and decorative seedheads.
⬚

Portulaca grandiflora
A spreading annual, up to 8in/20cm high, with red stems and fleshy green leaves. Single or double flowers in pink, red, yellow, or white appear throughout the summer. The Sundance Hybrids have large, semidouble or double flowers in a wide range of colors. (*See also P. oleracea, p.33.*)
⬚

PORTULACA GRANDIFLORA

SALVIA SCLAREA

Salvia sclarea (Clary)
A majestic biennial with eye-catching candelabras of pale pinkish lilac flowers that shoot up in its second year above large, wrinkled, highly aromatic leaves. Plants can reach over a 3ft/1m tall. The variety *turkestanica* has pink stems and pink-flecked white flowers.
⬚ Z5–9

Senecio cineraria
Although strictly a shrubby perennial, this is usually grown as an annual and a foliage plant. It forms 24in/60cm mounds of felted, deeply lobed leaves of silver-gray. Lower-growing 'Cirrus' is almost white – a striking contrast with other plants.
⬚ Z8–10

Silene coeli-rosa
(Rose of heaven)
A slender plant with gray-green leaves and long-stalked clusters of dainty pink flowers with white centers, borne in profusion in summer. Grows to about 20in/50cm. The flowers last well if cut for the house.
⬚

INDEX

ACKNOWLEDGMENTS

Picture research Sam Ruston
Illustrations Vanessa Luff
Additional illustrations Karen Cochrane
Index Hilary Bird

Dorling Kindersley would like to thank:
All staff at the RHS, in particular Susanne
Mitchell, Barbara Haynes and Karen Wilson
at Vincent Square; Candida Frith-Macdonald
for editorial assistance.

Photography
The publisher would also like to thank the
following for their kind permission to
reproduce their photographs:
(key: a=above, b=below, c=center, l=left,
r=right, t=top)

Peter Anderson Photography: 35b, 35tr
Eric Crichton Photos: 39bl
The Garden Picture Library: Christi Carter
37tl, Andrea Jones 44bl, Ron Sutherland 5bc,
9tl, 11bl, 25cl
John Glover: 4bl, 9br, 10br

Jerry Harpur: front cover cla, 6, Marcus
Harpur: 42cr
Andrew Lawson: back cover tl, 28, designer
David Magson 44br
S & O Mathews Photography: back cover c,
8bl, 31bl
Clive Nichols: designer Ann Frith front
cover tl, Green Farm Plants /Piet Oudolf back
cover tr, Ann Frith 4br, 7bl, David
Stevens/Julian Dowle 23br, Green Farm
Plants/ Piet Oudolf 16
Howard Rice: 2, 46
Harry Smith Collection: 5br, 15tl, 24bl, 29bl,
38
Jo Whitworth: 24bc, 39br
Rob Whitworth: front cover bl, 14b, 27bl

American Horticultural Society
Visit AHS at www.ahs.org or call them at
1-800-777-7931 ext. 10. Membership benefits
include The American Gardener magazine,
free admission to flower shows, the free seed
exchange, book services, and the Gardener's
Information Service.